WHY RAIN COMES FROM ABOVE

Explorations in Religious Imagination

ALSO BY DEVORA STEINMETZ

Punishment and Freedom:
The Rabbinic Construction of Criminal Law

2008

From Father to Son:
Kinship, Conflict, and Continuity in Genesis

1991

WHY RAIN COMES FROM ABOVE

Explorations in Religious Imagination
Devora Steinmetz

HADAR PRESS
New York

Copyright © 2024 by Devora Steinmetz

First edition

This book is licensed under a Creative Commons Attribution-NonCommercial-ShareAlike 4.0 International License

Library of Congress Control Number: 2023952675

The essay "Darkness Will Envelop Me" appeared in an earlier form in the online magazine thelehrhaus.com, on December 10, 2018.

Interior design by Rachel Jackson | binahdesign.com

HADAR PRESS
The Hadar Institute
212 West 93 Street
New York, New York 10025

In memory of those we lost on Simḥat Torah, 5784.

על אלה אני בוכיה

איכה א:טז

Hadar Press is grateful to

Rabbis Lauren and Jonathan Berkun
Rabbi Lisa Gelber
Rabbi Micah Peltz
Rabbi David Schuck
Rabbi Annie Tucker
Rabbi Marc and Rebecca Wolf

for their generous gifts in honor of Dr. Devora Steinmetz
and in support of the publication of this book

CONTENTS

- 1   Introduction: On Religious Imagination
- 9   Why Rain Comes From Above
- 33   Darkness Will Envelop Me
- 49   Work and Its Purposes
- 75   To Know and Be Known
- 99   God's Eternal Enemy
- 125   The Hidden and the Revealed
- 155   Acknowledgements
- 157   Notes on Sources and Suggestions for Further Reading

INTRODUCTION: ON RELIGIOUS IMAGINATION

"So they told these stories because they didn't know what *really* makes rain fall?"

I was teaching a course on Ta'anit, a talmudic tractate about how to respond to lack of rainfall and other disasters. The tractate includes an unusual number of stories, especially in its third chapter, which is almost entirely narrative. It depicts a world in which rain is divinely given, and in which it is sent down or withheld in response to human behavior. Each of these premises—that rain is directly sent by God and that rainfall is God's response to human behavior—stands outside of the scientific perspective that we learn in school and that is our default way of thinking about the world. Hence, my student's question: Did they tell all of these stories as a way to try to make sense of a world that they didn't understand?

I don't think that that is why they told these stories. More importantly, I don't think that that's how we should *read* these stories. This book is an attempt to offer a way of reading and responding to stories such as the ones that my student found so foreign to his way of thinking.

Many of us are taught—or simply assume—that biblical and rabbinic stories are to be taken as literal truth. This assumption leaves us two choices: to accept these literal truths or to reject these stories as inconsistent with our understanding of the world. Assertions and aspirations articulated in our *tefillot* pose similar challenges. If we don't *really* anticipate the rebuilding of the Temple and the reinstitution of animal sacrifice, what should we do? We can say those words anyway and ignore or live with the dissonance between our words and our beliefs, or we can choose to omit those words. Or, in the case of *tefillah*, we can put them in past tense, so that they describe a past reality rather than articulating a wish for an anticipated future.

Alternatively, if we are committed to the traditional words but can't accept their literal meaning, we can reinterpret them, in particular by understanding them metaphorically. Our own selves are understood to be a sanctuary, for example. Or God's threat to withhold rain in the second paragraph of Shema (Deuteronomy 11:13-17) is understood to refer to the climate crisis brought about by human misdeeds that are destructive to the environment.

Each of these strategies reflects different and important stances toward our tradition, toward how we understand the nature of prayer, and toward how we navigate dissonance. Each is deployed, though in radically different degrees, across the spectrum of Jewish communities. And each is reflected in contemporary Siddurim, in their texts and their translations and in their comments and commentaries. The goal of this book is to offer an alternative to these strategies for relating to our sacred texts—to invite readers into an exploration of religious imagination.

By religious imagination I mean allowing ourselves to step inside the stories, images, and teachings that our texts and *tefillot* offer, and open ourselves to the experiences and awareness that make themselves available to us. We engage similar kinds of imagination all the time, in particular when we become absorbed in reading a novel or enter into the world of the characters in a television series. We do this perhaps more readily in those situations because we know that these things are not real—their genre signals this to us upfront—and because they do not make a strong claim on us. We can easily step into their imagined reality and step back out—though of course a great piece of literature or gripping series may, in fact, continue to have a hold on us. We may continue to feel that we know the characters, we may continue to care about them; our world may have been broadened, our consciousness may have been aroused, our values may have shifted.

It can be more difficult to allow ourselves this kind of absorption in the sacred texts that we study and the prayers that we recite. We might assume that the claims of these texts and *tefillot* are meant to be taken as propositional truths. We may have been told that this is so, or we may know others who believe that this is so, and we might feel resistance toward being drawn into beliefs that we do not share. Additionally, the stakes are higher: these texts and prayers make a claim on us in ways that literature, film, and television do not. These are canonical texts, texts that are foundational to a normative tradition, and so we cannot just walk into imaginative engagement with them and then walk out, the way we can (or feel that we can) choose to do with a novel or a show. Also, like the texts about rain that my student asked about, they come from a past world that, it is immediately apparent to us, holds assumptions that are different from our own, that are foreign to us, while much of the literature that we read and the shows that we watch are written for *us*, now. They offer to draw us into a world that is fictional but familiar, while our traditional texts threaten to draw us into a different, at times alien, world.

But leaving what is familiar and entering the unfamiliar, even sometimes foreign or strange, invites us into ways of thinking and feeling and experiencing that broaden us, that take us outside of what we already think and feel and know. We enter into imaginative worlds that draw us into stories, encounters, and experiences that are different from those in our everyday world. And these open us to new ways of thinking and feeling. We live ourselves into these stories, and they continue to live in us as we step back from study or prayer or ritual into our everyday lives.

The role of imagination in religious study, prayer, and ritual has been emphasized in a variety of religious traditions. The Spiritual Exercises of the Ignatian Catholic tradition, for example, call on the imagination both to contemplate the world from the divine perspective, thus cultivating divine qualities such as compassion and understanding, as well as to enter into biblical stories, experiencing them with the imagination and, ultimately, participating in them. And contemporary Evangelical Christians as well as members of other religious traditions use imagination, in ways described in the work of anthropologist Tanya Luhrmann, to create a felt sense of God's presence in their lives.

Within Jewish tradition, some Hasidic teachers have recommended using visualization or other forms of imaginative evocation as a portal to experiences such as standing in God's presence during prayer. Such experiences are not accessible to our physical senses, nor can they be accessed through abstract reasoning or rational theology. Keenly aware of these challenges, Rabbi Kalonymus Kalman Shapira, for example, offers instruction to a young student who finds himself unable to access the experience of standing in the divine presence when praying because the *idea* of God is too abstract to evoke such an intense experience.

Rabbi Shapira suggests to his student that he temporarily set aside the Maimonidean ban on visualizing God and actively conjure an image of himself standing before God's throne and pleading directly to God about his spiritual and physical needs (Benei Maḥshavah Tovah, pp. 18-20). Other visualizations are recommended for different challenges, including those relating to a student's very nature: if a student can't achieve the level of piety that he aspires to reach, he is enjoined to visualize himself as a pious person, to *see* in his imagination the greatness of his soul (Tzav ve-Zeruz 24; see also 2).

But imagination, for Rabbi Shapira, is not limited to calling up visual imagery. In one of the homilies that he wrote during his final months in the Warsaw Ghetto, Rabbi Shapira suggests that saying a word, in fact merely a pronoun, can both express and evoke a rich religious experience. Basing his teaching on the biblical story of Judah approaching Joseph, who is posing as an Egyptian vizier threatening to enslave Benjamin, Rabbi Shapira notes the repeated variation between second- and third-person address to the person whom Judah is beseeching. In our prayers, Rabbi Shapira points out, we address God in second person, as "you," and saying the word "you" always presupposes that there is someone present to whom you are speaking and, moreover, that you are present before them. Even if we enter prayer not feeling God's presence or not feeling like we are able to be present before God—that is, if we begin prayer in a stance in which God is a distant third-person—the words that we say expressing our desire to love and fear God, and the way in which we address God as "you," evoke an experience of being drawn to God and of being present in God's presence (Eish Kodesh, VaYigash 5702 - 1941).

Common to all of these approaches is the recognition that imagination makes accessible to us a range of experiences and depth of understanding that may not be available through rational thought alone, and that the work of imagining can transform us. The essays in this book are gathered under the subheading of "religious imagination," a conception that shares the core recognition of the approaches that I've briefly reviewed but also diverges from them in a significant way. I share with these approaches a recognition of the rich experiences and understanding that imagination makes possible, but my approach is not grounded in the assumption that what is imagined is also literally true, that imagination is a way to access and develop or strengthen *belief* in the propositional sense of the word. Rather, imagination in this book relates to an *as if* experience.

Introduction

Returning to the last example from Rabbi Shapira, the approach that I am taking brackets the question of belief. Whether or not your (rational) theology allows that there is a personal God before whom you are standing in prayer, what happens if you just say the word "you" and actually enter into the experience of saying "you"? What happens if you allow yourself the imaginative experience of being in God's presence, of talking directly to God? Or, returning to the wish for the restoration of the Temple and sacrificial worship in our prayers, what happens if we bracket the propositional value of that statement ("I really do want and anticipate a future Beit ha-Mikdash and the return of animal sacrifice") and imagine ourselves into an experience of standing in the Temple, crowded and noisy and bloody, and offering a sacrifice to God? Or, to return to my student's question, what happens if we allow ourselves to imagine rain being sent by God, by a God who is intimately involved in and responsive to the behavior of human beings?

Religious texts draw us into engagement with things that are bigger than ourselves; things that are cosmic, eternal, covenantal; concerns about justice and ethics and responsibility; and conceptions of how we might think about our lives and about our world and about God. Imaginative engagement in religious texts and practices heightens awareness of our mundane experiences, layering them with significance and meaning. It can transform our relationship to the world around us and awaken us to the ethical commitments to which we are called. And it can give us ways of thinking about things that, despite all that we know, we don't fully understand.

Each of the essays in this book explores biblical and rabbinic texts, and sometimes practices, and invites the reader into the imaginative space created by deep engagement with these texts and practices. The first essay, "Why Rain Comes From Above," takes on the challenge posed by my student's question. Taking as its starting point a *midrash* that asserts that God deliberately chose to provide water to the world by sending it down from the heavens, the essay weaves together biblical and rabbinic texts that present the mundane experience of rainfall as an invitation to imagine a dynamic world animated by God's call to justice.

The next essay, "Darkness Will Envelop Me," considers two versions of a talmudic story about Adam and the first winter, in conversation with talmudic passages about the practice of lighting Hanukkah candles. Each of these texts is a *thick* text—each evokes one or more additional texts that live within it, and several of these texts capture, by implication or explicitly, opposing experiences or realities or practices. This layering and complexity of meaning are expressed in the simple act of Hanukkah candle-lighting—a practice that invites us into the imaginative experience of living, along with the first human being and all human beings, with the terrifying and hopeful interplay of darkness and light.

The following two essays focus on core themes in the Israelites' move from enslavement to redemption in the book of Exodus. The first of these, "Work and Its Purposes," picks up on the relationship between stories and practices. It explores the different kinds of work that the Israelites did in Egypt and during their wilderness journey, and considers ways in which the practices of Shabbat call us into stories of enslavement and redemption. The next essay, "To Know and Be Known," looks at different kinds of knowledge and different ways of knowing. The story of becoming God's people in the book of Exodus is an unfolding of ways of knowing, as the Israelites come to know God and strive to know how to walk in the world. Knowledge, it turns out, is deeply connected to empathy and compassion, qualities of imagination that must inform human behavior and that can enable God to be present amongst the people whom God has delivered from their oppressors.

The final two essays explore additional ways that our texts invite us to imagine God's involvement in the world as well as our own responsibility, returning us to core themes of the opening essay about rain. "God's Eternal Enemy" suggests that Amalek can be understood to represent a primordial force of evil that continues to challenge God's dominion. The story of Amalek allows us to imagine the world as a place in which divine justice and compassion are not fully realized, a place that is a battleground between good and evil, and in which goodness does not always prevail. In such a world, our declarations of God's kingship are anticipatory, describing an imagined and hoped-for future state, rather than a proposition about the world as it is. And in such a world we are called upon to take sides in this cosmic battle, pushing back the forces of evil, making room for more goodness, expanding God's dominion.

"The Hidden and the Revealed" focuses on an enigmatic biblical verse and its implications for conceptions of human responsibility, individual and communal. Like the texts discussed in the essay about darkness, this verse is a particularly thick text: both an anomaly of orthography and the ambiguity of the verse's referents invite multiple alternative readings and understandings. The verse and its rabbinic interpretations offer competing conceptions of what it means to be a responsible human being and to live in a society that strives to be good, and of the relationship between what we know and what we are held responsible for. And rabbinic commentary on the related concept of *areivut* invites us to imagine ways we are intertwined in a web of responsibility with the communities of which we are a part.

This final essay instantiates most palpably a core feature of the textual explorations in each of the essays: details—of structure, of word choice, of grammar and syntax, and even of the way the words of the Torah are written—encapsulate meaning. Careful reading, paying close attention, noticing the ways in which our texts speak and, sometimes, the ambiguities that our texts incorporate are entry points into imaginative worlds that can transform us.

The essays in this book do not aim to provide a roadmap for how to engage in religious imagination. Rather, they afford opportunities for exploration, opening for the reader a portal into the imaginative world of selected texts and practices. They offer an invitation back into the literal – not to take the literal meaning as propositional truth, to be accepted or rejected, and not to avoid the literal by translating it into metaphor. The literal, here, beckons the reader to engage imaginatively, to enter into an *as if* experience and to discover new meanings and understandings. These essays, then, are explorations – they invite the reader on journeys of imaginative exploration and, I hope, encourage the reader to explore more broadly, in study, prayer, and practice, what it might mean to engage in the adventure of religious imagination.

WHY RAIN COMES FROM ABOVE

> Thus did the land drink at the beginning:
> "And a spring would come up from the land
> and water all of the face of the earth" (Genesis 2:6).
> And the Blessed Holy One changed his mind
> so that the land would drink only from above.
>
> Bereishit Rabbah 13:9

RAIN IS PART of the natural world in which we live; it is a phenomenon that we take as a given. We may live in a place in which there are rainy days all year round or in a place in which there are rainy seasons and seasons in which there is no rain. We may do agricultural work or related work that makes us acutely aware of when the rain falls and whether there is enough or too little or too much rain, or we may experience rain as nothing more than something that we need to attend to in order to know whether to grab an umbrella on our way out the door. But we all take for granted that rain comes down from the sky, and that the earth gets its water from the rain that falls from above.

The *midrash* invites us to pause, take notice, and choose *not* to take for granted that the way things are is the way things have to be. What if rain *didn't* come from above? What if the water on which the earth depends came from elsewhere? What if we suspend our presumption that the water on which the earth depends comes down in the form of rain and allow ourselves to be surprised by the fact that it *does*? And then what if we asked: *Why is it that way?*

WHY RAIN COMES FROM ABOVE

The *midrash* beckons us into a world in which the physical reality is not simply a natural phenomenon; rather, it is a reflection of something important about the world in which we live. Rain, in such a world, is imagined as an intentional choice by a creator who could have made other choices – indeed, the *midrash* claims, by a creator who initially *did* make a different choice. By calling our attention to rain as a divine *choice*, the *midrash* asks us to consider what difference it makes that our world is watered by rain. What can we, human beings who live in a world that is watered by rain, come to understand once we stop to notice that God made a deliberate decision that rain should come from above?

The *midrash* makes its claim by citing a verse from the beginning of the creation story in Genesis 2, which describes how the earth was watered at the beginning of time. The verse says that water *came up* from the land. The *midrash* asserts that this terrestrial upflowing of water was God's original plan for how the land would be watered but that God later changed God's mind and decided that the earth would receive water, instead, *from above*.

The *midrash* will go on to suggest four reasons for this change, and thus it offers a reflection on why it is a good thing for the earth to receive its water from rain, which comes from above. We will turn to these reasons later. First, we will look at the verse that the *midrash* cites and notice that the *midrash* is offering an exegesis of this verse. The exegesis focuses on a difficult word in the verse, a word that has been subject to a variety of interpretations from ancient to modern times. We will consider the significance of this verse in the context of the story of creation and of the larger narrative of the Torah, and then return to the *midrash* which cites this verse, to the reasons that the *midrash* gives for God's change of plan, and to the meanings of rain that the *midrash* helps us to see.

Here is the verse again, this time with the obscure Hebrew word left untranslated:

> And (or—But) an *eid* would come up from the land
> and water all of the face of the earth.

The first difficulty in understanding the verse is the word "*eid*," which appears only one other time in the entire Tanakh, in the notoriously difficult book of Job (36:27). Given the rarity of this word, we can only conjecture about its meaning from the contexts in which it appears. Since our verse describes the *eid* as going up from the land, we might imagine that the word signifies some kind of spring or other terrestrial upflowing of subterranean waters.

But an additional difficulty arises from a consideration of this verse in its biblical context. Here is the verse along with the verses immediately preceding and immediately following it:

> ⁵And no shrub of the field was yet on the land
> and no grass of the field had yet grown,
> because the Lord God had not brought rain on the land
> and there was no human being to work the earth.
>
> ⁶And (or—But) an *eid* would go up from the land
> and water all the face of the earth.
>
> ⁷And the Lord God formed the human being
> of dust from the earth
> and he breathed into his nostrils the breath of life,
> and the human being became a living being.
>
> *Genesis 2:5-7*

The first of these verses describes the state of things at the beginning of the story of the world's coming into being in the second chapter of Genesis. It is a beautifully structured verse, with each half of the verse including two parallel segments. The first half of the verse describes the state of the earth before the events that will follow in this narrative, and the second half of the verse explains why it was that the land at that time was barren of plant life. Two causes are mentioned in this second half of the verse: the lack of rain ("because the Lord God had not brought rain on the land") and the lack of a human being ("and there was no human being to work the earth").

The following two verses correlate with the two things that this first verse has mentioned as missing. Verse 6 tells how the earth was watered, and verse 7 describes the creation of the human being. But the neatness of this structure is what raises the second difficulty in understanding the meaning of the word "*eid.*" If verse 5 describes the two things that are lacking but necessary in order for the land to bring forth vegetation, and verse 7 tells how the second of these two things came to be, then we would expect the intervening verse to tell how the first of the two missing things came to be. That is, if verse 5 tells us that "there was no human being to work the earth," and verse 7 tells us that God created the human being, then we would expect that verse 6 would talk about the introduction of rain, the other thing that verse 5 tells us has been missing: "the Lord God had not brought rain on the land."

But it is difficult to understand verse 6 as talking about the introduction of rain. First, if the verse is describing rain, then it should describe the water source as coming *down* upon the land. Yet the verse describes the *eid* as going *up* from the land. Some commentaries and translations address this problem by interpreting *eid* as a mist or cloud which rises from the land only to fall again as rain (see Rashi and Onkelos) – and many present-day biblical translations retain this interpretation in rendering *eid* as "mist." But this interpretation seems forced, attempting to make verse 6 consistent with the expectation that verse 5 has engendered. It assumes that verse 6 is telling us that the rain that the preceding verse says did not yet exist has now been introduced. But it is odd that verse 6, if announcing the advent of rain, would do so by focusing on an element of the water cycle that is secondary to rain.

Second, if verse 6 *is* describing rain, then *eid* is not the word that we would expect to find. As noted, it is not clear what the word *eid* means, but if the Torah means to tell us that now God has brought rain, we should expect it to use the noun *matar* or the verb *himtir*, as it does in verse 5 ("the Lord God had not brought rain"—*lo himtir*) and elsewhere when the Torah talks about rain.

And finally, the form of the verb in verse 6 suggests that we do not have something new here, but rather that there is a continuous phenomenon in place. "An *eid* would go up (*ya'aleh*) from the land" does not suggest that *now* God creates the *eid*, as God will create the human being in verse 7, but rather that the *eid* continues to go up from the land as it has until now. In fact, verses 7, 8, and 9 each begin with a verb the subject of which is the Lord God—God formed, God planted, God caused to grow—and this highlights the fact that verse 6 does not say that God created a new source of water.

It seems then that the Torah, contrary to the expectation set up by verse 5, is not telling us in verse 6 that now there is rain on the earth. Rather, the Torah seems to be saying that, initially, there was something *other* than rain that watered the earth. *Ve-eid*, then, would best be rendered not as "*And* an *eid*" but as "*But* an *eid*"—that is, there was no rain on the land (v. 5), *but* there was something else that watered the earth at this point in time (v. 6). The garden that is about to be planted in Eden (v. 8), the Torah is telling us, will be watered not by rain, which comes *down* to the earth, but by something that comes *up* from the earth, the *eid*. This water that flows or gushes up from the earth is most probably the source of the river introduced in verse 10, which waters the garden and separates into four tributaries that flow outward to water the outside world.

But, if this is the case, why does verse 5 mention rain at all? Why is it important to anticipate the future dependence of the earth on rain, when in the story that this verse introduces there is no need for rain at all, given the *eid* that waters the garden and the surrounding lands? And how can we understand the parallel in verse 5 between the anticipated existence of rain and the anticipated existence of a human being who will work the earth?

Umberto Cassuto, the masterful twentieth-century Bible scholar, offers a compelling suggestion. Verse 5, according to Cassuto, is not describing the elements of how the world worked at the beginning of time, when the human being was about to be created and placed in the Garden of Eden. Rather, verse 5 is anticipating the post-Edenic world; it describes how the world will work after Adam, who is about to be created, is banished from the Garden (Genesis 3:23-24). In other words, it describes the world in which the rest of the biblical narrative will unfold, the world that the Torah understands to be the world in which we live, not the idyllic world of Eden.

Thus, according to Cassuto, verse 5 is describing a world in which human beings will live by means of agriculture, in which they will plow and sow and reap "the grass of the field" (compare 2:5 with 3:18), and in which they will be vulnerable to the vagaries of rainfall. This is not the world of Eden, in which the human being needed merely to pick the fruits of the trees that God had planted, and in which the trees were watered by an ever-present stream.

I would characterize the difference between these two worlds as the difference between a pre-moral universe and a world of moral choice. Eden is a pre-moral universe, a world in which the human being does not yet have the ability to choose between good and evil. The post-Edenic world, on the other hand, is a world of moral choice; the human being has eaten the fruit of the Tree of Knowledge of Good and Evil, and has been thrust into a condition of moral autonomy. In that state, the choices that a person makes to do good or to do evil are responded to, are rewarded or punished – and, in the Torah, the main vehicle of reward and punishment is rain.

In fact, the very first time that we encounter rain in the Torah, it is a vehicle of destruction. The first thing that God rains down is the waters of the flood (Genesis 7:4), brought as a response to human corruption. In words that recall the story of the creation of the human being and the expulsion from Eden in Genesis 2 and 3, God sees the evil (*ra*—as in the Tree of Knowledge of Good and Evil from which the human being was forbidden to eat, 2:9, 17) of the human being, that the creations (*yetzer*—as in *va-yitzer*, the forming of the human being from the dust of the earth, 2:7) of his heart are only evil, and God grieves (*va-yit'atzev*—as in *itzavon*, the sorrow that both the woman and the man will experience in the aftermath of their violation of God's command, 3:16-17). In response, God determines to destroy the world by means of rain.

Strikingly, the next time that God sends down rain, it is also used to destroy. The second narrative in which the verb *lehamtir* appears is the story of the destruction of Sodom. In this case, God rains down not water but brimstone and fire (Genesis 19:24). And the third narrative in which the verb appears is the account of the plagues against Egypt; the seventh plague is the raining down of hail (Exodus 9:18). So the first three stories in which God causes something to rain down from the heavens exemplify the idea of rain as a vehicle of judgment, and, notably, in each of these three cases what is rained down is something that destroys, not something that, as we might expect of rain, brings life to the earth.

In fact, there is only one other story in the Torah in which God rains down something from the heavens. In this case, it *is* something that sustains life, but it is not water. It is the manna that God rains down for the Israelites in the wilderness. While the manna is not exactly a vehicle of judgment, it is sent down in response to the Israelites' complaining about having left Egypt, and it is sent down along with a series of expectations and demands. When God announces to Moses that God will send down (*mamtir*) the manna, God makes it clear that its purpose is to test whether the people will follow God's instruction (Exodus 16:4).

Cassuto's characterization of rain, then, is certainly correct. Rain in the Torah—that is, *matar*, something that is sent down from the heavens—is not a neutral phenomenon. It is a tool of judgment, whether a response to human (mis)behavior—as in the stories of the flood, the destruction of Sodom, and the plague of hail—or a means of instruction involving rules and demands—as in the story of the manna. Cassuto's novel insight is that rain is only appropriate for and necessary in the post-Edenic world. And thus, the verse in which rain is first mentioned, Genesis 2:5, is anticipating an essential part of the Torah's vision for the world into which Adam will step once he becomes a morally autonomous human being.

THE PROMISED LAND

A brief passage in the book of Deuteronomy offers a vivid contrast between a land that obtains its water from rainfall and a land that has water ready to hand from a terrestrial source:

> [10]For the land to which you are coming
> to take possession of it—
> it is not like the land of Egypt which you left, where you sow
> your seed and water it with your foot,
> like a vegetable garden.
>
> [11]But the land into which you are crossing over
> to take possession of it—
> it is a land of mountains and valleys;
> it drinks water from the rain of the heavens.
>
> [12]It is a land that the Lord your God seeks out;
> always the eyes of the Lord your God are upon it
> from the beginning of the year until the end of the year.
>
> *Deuteronomy 11:10-12*

Here, the contrast is between the land of Egypt and the promised land. While the land into which the Israelites will cross is dependent on rain for its water, the land of Egypt is watered by streams fed by the Nile (hence, the most likely explanation of "water it with your foot" relates to controlling the flow of irrigation channels).

The first verse in this passage compares the way in which the land of Egypt is watered to the way in which a garden is watered. The reference to a garden recalls the Garden of Eden; Egypt, the verse is suggesting, is like the Garden of Eden in not being dependent on rain. In fact, in Genesis 13, when Lot separates from Abram and chooses the fertile Jordan valley, we are told that the place is "well-watered... like the garden of the Lord, like the land of Egypt" (13:10). (For "the garden of the Lord" as synonymous with Eden, see Isaiah 51:3; see also Ezekiel 31:8-9.) "Well-watered" (*mashkeh*) is based on the same root that is used in the verse describing the garden-like Egypt in Deuteronomy (*ve-hishkita*, 11:10), and that describes the *eid*'s watering of the earth earlier in Genesis (*ve-hishkah*, 2:6). Both in the Lot story, then, and in the Deuteronomy verse, Egypt is compared to a well-watered garden, and in the Lot story, the fertile Jordan valley is compared to the garden-like Egypt. But, the Lot passage notes, this was before God destroyed Sodom (13:10), whose "people are evil and very sinful before the Lord" (13:13).

The implication of this cluster of verses is that a place that receives its water from terrestrial sources, that is well-watered and not dependent on rain, is a place that is not the focus of God's attention. It is not a place on which God makes moral demands. Egypt, after all, only becomes the focus of God's attention when the Egyptians abuse God's chosen people. Sodom will be destroyed only when the cry of the abused is so great that God goes down to see how terrible the deeds of the Sodomites are (18:20-21). Eden is not an *im*moral place like Egypt and Sodom, but it is a *pre*-moral place. It is a place in which the human being is asked to follow God's command, but it is not a place in which human beings are expected to make moral judgments—the human being, in Eden, has not yet eaten of the Tree of Knowledge of Good and Evil and does not yet have the capacity for moral discernment. So the Deuteronomy passage is saying that Egypt is like Eden, a place in which you can expect the land to be well-watered whether or not you make moral choices.

But the promised land is different. "Always the eyes of the Lord your God are upon it," we are told. "It is a land that the Lord your God seeks out." *Lidrosh*—"to seek"—has a range of connotations, several of which are relevant here. The word can have a forensic meaning, as it does elsewhere in Deuteronomy where the community is enjoined to investigate reports of misdeeds on the part of community members: "you shall search out (*ve-darashta*) and investigate and inquire" (Deuteronomy 13:15; see also 17:4 and 19:18). It can also mean to demand or require, as it does, for example, in the famous verse from Micah: "…what is good and what the Lord requires (*doreish*) of you" (6:8). And it can also suggest care, as in "no one cares (*doreish*) for my soul" (Psalm 142:5).

These meanings are all related, of course. God has a special relationship with the land into which the people are about to cross over: God cares for it, and so makes demands of it, and therefore inquires as to how its inhabitants are acting. God looks down upon it at all times. And this combination of care, demand, and inquiry is connected with the land's dependency on rain. *This* land, the Deuteronomy passage is saying, is a place whose inhabitants are expected to act in accordance with God's demands and whose fertility depends on the behavior of its inhabitants.

In fact, the passage continues with the verses that we know as the second paragraph of the Shema:

> [13]It will be that,
> if you listen to my commandments that I command you,
> to love the Lord your God
> and to serve him with all your heart and with all your soul,
> [14]I will give the rain of your land in its season....
>
> [16]Beware lest your hearts be enticed
> and you turn aside and worship other gods and bow to them.
> [17]The anger of the Lord will be kindled against you,
> and he will shut up (*ve-atzar*) the heavens,
> and there will not be rain,
> and the earth will not give its produce. ...

The distinction between Egypt and the promised land, then, is the distinction between a world that gets its water from an *eid* and a world that is dependent on rain. In the land into which the Israelites are about to cross, these verses tell us, rain will come only if the people fulfill God's commandments; if they do not, God will shut up the heavens and no rain will come down to the earth.

WITHHOLDING RAIN

But what kind of misbehavior will cause the withholding of rain? In the Deuteronomy passage, rain will be withheld if the people turn away and worship other gods. But each of the Talmudim includes a passage about what will cause the withholding of rain, and the differences between these lists of causes and the biblical passage are striking. Here is what causes lack of rain according to the Talmud Yerushalmi:

WHY RAIN COMES FROM ABOVE

> On account of four sins rain is withheld (*ne'etzarin*):
> the sin of idol worshippers
> and those who engage in illicit sexual relationships
> and those who spill blood
> and those who pledge in public and do not give.
>
> *Yerushalmi Ta'anit* 3:3/66c

Using the language of the biblical passage—*ne'etzarin* ("withheld") is from the same root as *ve-atzar* ("shut up") in Deuteronomy 11:17—the Yerushalmi offers four reasons for drought. The first is the reason given in the Deuteronomy passage, idol worship. But a quick scan of the list reveals that the Yerushalmi has incorporated idol worship into a familiar group of three sins that are considered to be the most serious offenses. And then there is a fourth behavior that just doesn't seem to belong. In other words, a person reading this list would immediately recognize the "big three" sins of idol worship, illicit sexual relationships, and murder—but then what is that fourth sin doing there? By offering an expected list of the most heinous crimes, led off by the sin that the Deuteronomy passage explicitly mentions, the Yerushalmi passage seems to be highlighting the entirely *un*expected addition to this list—the at-first-glance very moderate offense of not fulfilling one's pledge. *This*, the passage seems to be saying, is a truly egregious offense that merits God's refusal to send down life-giving rain.

The parallel text in the Talmud Bavli offers a longer list of possible causes for the withholding of rain, each cause proposed by a different sage. Notably, the sin of idolatry does not appear here at all, and neither do the other two most-serious crimes: illicit sexual relationships and murder. Over the course of a lengthy passage, the Bavli offers seven statements beginning with the words "Rain is withheld only on account of," again using the biblical word that signifies God's decision not to send down rain. Here are the first and last of the relatively unremarkable misdeeds that are mentioned:

> Said Rav Ḥisda:
> Rain is withheld (*ne'etzarin*) only on account of
> neglecting priestly gifts and tithes. ...

> And said Rabbi Yoḥanan:
> Rain is withheld (*ne'etzarin*) only on account of
> those who pledge charity in public and do not give.
>
> Bavli Ta'anit 7b, 8b

The last of these reasons is identical to the surprising last reason that is given in the Yerushalmi—failure to pay one's charity pledge. The first is similar, failure to pay one's obligatory dues to the priests, the Levites, and the indigent.

And so the Talmudim have retained the biblical notion of rain being an instrument of judgment, of the giving or withholding of rain as a response to human obedience or sinfulness. But the Talmudim have shifted the focus from turning away from God and worshiping other gods to failing to give the gifts that one is obligated to give to those who are in need.

A different passage from the Yerushalmi can help make sense of why these particular misdeeds are seen to cause rain to be withheld. This passage appears in the context of a discussion about the Mishnah's teaching that if, at a certain point in the rainy season, rain has not yet come, *yeḥidim* (individuals) initiate a series of fasts (Mishnah Ta'anit 1:4). The Talmud tells several stories about individuals who are asked to pray for rain, among which is the following:

> A certain person would set aside his tithes
> as they are supposed to be.
>
> Rabbi Mana said to him:
> "Rise and say: 'I have removed the holy things from the house.'"
>
> Yerushalmi Ta'anit 1:4/64b

The passage is referring to a declaration that Deuteronomy dictates should be made by the person who distributes their tithes:

> [13]I have removed the holy things from the house,
> and I have given them to the Levite and to the stranger,
> to the orphan and to the widow....

> ¹⁵Look down from your holy habitation, from the heavens,
> and bless your people Israel
> and the earth that you have given us. ...
>
> *Deuteronomy 26:13, 15*

The declaration links the distribution of tithes to God sending down a blessing from God's heavenly abode. And God is asked to look down from the heavens at God's people Israel. This image recalls the portrayal earlier in Deuteronomy, where the promised land is described as a place that God looks down upon, that God watches, and where God's seeking out of the land is linked to the gift of rain. In this later Deuteronomy passage, God is *implored* to look, and what God will see is that the person making the declaration has given a tithe of his produce to those who are in need and that the people of Israel are in need of blessing. In the talmudic story, it is this text that is used as a prayer for rain, and it is the person who properly tithes who is designated as the individual who can pray for rain.

And so the shift from Deuteronomy 11's focus on idolatry as the cause for the withholding of rain to the Talmudim's focus on failing to pay one's pledges or give one's tithes is not as stark as it at first appears. As it turns out, the notion of tithing as meriting God's looking down and bestowing blessing appears in Deuteronomy as well. From the perspective of the Yerushalmi passage, Deuteronomy 26:15 is asking God—or can be deployed to ask God—to cease withholding rain: to look down, recognize that the people have shared the blessing that they have been given, and shower down blessing from the heavens. The idea that sharing the blessings that God bestows is an invitation to God to shower down blessing is echoed in the Talmudim's comments that failing to share God's blessings by tithing or giving the charity that one has pledged causes the withholding of rain. (Notably, in Sifrei Devarim 40 the word *doreish* in Deuteronomy 11:12 is understood to refer to a *specific* demand—the requirement to set aside ḥallah, terumah, and tithes.)

FROM JUDGMENT TO JUSTICE

Having looked at the significance of the *eid* in the Garden of Eden and the meaning of the contrast between water that comes from the earth and rain that comes from above, let's return to the midrashic passage with which we began. The *midrash* asserts that God changed the way the earth would receive its water; at first watered by the *eid*, the earth now receives its water from above. Why did God change God's plan? The *midrash* offers four reasons:

> Rav Ḥanan of Tzipori said
> in the name of Rabbi Shmuel son of Naḥman:
> On account of four things God changed his mind
> so that the land would only drink from above—
> on account of strongmen
> and in order to cleanse bad dews
> and so that the high might drink like the low
> and so that all would direct their eyes upward,
> as it is written: "To set on high those who are low" (Job 5:11).
>
> *Bereishit Rabbah 13:9*
> *(parallel in Yerushalmi Ta'anit 3:3/66c)*

I want to focus on three of these four explanations, the three that talk about people, setting aside the second explanation, which talks about the salutary effect of the water cycle on the purity of rainwater.

The first explanation suggests that water that is available from a terrestrial source is vulnerable to "strongmen." People who are more powerful, whether physically strong or better situated socially, can take more than their fair share of water. If you live upstream or you are powerful or you are privileged in some other way, you can siphon water from a terrestrial source such as a river or stream, leaving little or no water for those who are less well-situated. Rain, in contrast, cannot be controlled by those who are powerful.

The third explanation focuses on the geographical location of those who need water. Here the *midrash* seems to be working with the Deuteronomy 11 passage. Note the word "drink," used in the third explanation as well as in the introduction to all four explanations. This word echoes Deuteronomy 11:11:

> But the land into which you are crossing over
> to take possession of it—
> it is a land of mountains and valleys;
> it drinks water from the rain of the heavens.

The word "drinks" (*tishteh*) can be construed in two ways: it can be third-person feminine, referring to the land, as it has been translated here. Alternatively, it can be second-person masculine, in which case the end of the verse should be translated "you drink water from the rain of the heavens." Our *midrash* includes both of these possibilities. The introduction says that God decided that *the land* should drink from above. The third explanation says that *the people* drink, those who live up high like those who live down low.

The reference to people who live high up and low down also echoes the Deuteronomy verse. "It is a land of mountains and valleys" is a geographical observation that aligns with the land's dependence on rain. The *midrash* works with this observation and transforms it into an ethical concern. God chooses to bring rain *so that* those who live on high—on the mountains—will have access to water just as do those who live below—in the valleys. Water that is available from a terrestrial source, in contrast, would be readily available to those who live on low land but not to those who live up high.

The third explanation for rain, then, is consonant with the first explanation. According to both, God decides to make water available by means of rain so that water will be equally available to everyone. In the first explanation, rain avoids the possibility of control by those who are powerful; in the third explanation, rain avoids the unequal access that is the consequence of people living in different geographical locations. In both, God's decision to provide water via rain is an ethical choice.

A subtle shift has occurred between the Deuteronomy passage on which this *midrash* is based and the *midrash* itself. In the Deuteronomy passage, as elsewhere in the Tanakh, rain is an instrument of *judgment*. In the *midrash*, rain is an instrument of *justice*. The *midrash*, in other words, is retaining the biblical notion that rain is intimately connected to the choice to do good or evil. But in the *midrash* rain itself is a vehicle for the doing of good—it comes in a way that prevents people from using their power to take advantage of others, and it comes in a way that gives everyone an equal share.

The *midrash*'s final reason for rain is "so that all would direct their eyes upward." Looking upward can have many resonances. It can suggest dependence; God sends down rain from above so that people will recognize their vulnerability and their dependence on God. In fact, in the only story in the Torah in which God rains down something that sustains rather than destroys life, what is rained down has this purpose, among others. The manna, we noted above, is sent as a way to test whether the people will follow God's instruction. Its appearance is also connected with revelation, the visible manifestation of God's glory (Exodus 16:7). In Deuteronomy, the manna is portrayed also as cultivating an awareness of dependence on God; it is set in opposition to the possibility that people will imagine that what they possess has been gained by their own power (Deuteronomy 8:11-17). Directing one's eyes upward, then, means awareness of being in God's presence and awareness that it is God who sustains life and who is the source of the blessings that human beings enjoy.

In addition to pointing to this awareness, the final explanation of why God brings water from above might also relate to the first two explanations that we have looked at; the *midrash*'s statement that "all" look upward suggests a kind of equalizing of rich and poor, powerful and weak, well-situated and poorly-situated, *all* of whom are forced to see themselves as needing God to send down rain. Imagining everyone looking upward creates an image of all people, large and small, high and low, reduced to the same size relative to the vast height of the heavens.

The passage cited from Job at the end of the *midrash* supports the notion that this final explanation sees rain as an equalizing mechanism. Here is the quoted phrase along with the verse that precedes it:

> [10]Who gives rain on the face of the land
> and sends water on the face of the fields,
> [11]to set on high those who are low....
>
> *Job 5:10-11*

These verses suggest that God's gift of rain raises up those who are low, most literally referring to rain as a life-giving force that brings hope and sustenance to the destitute. But the passage goes on to speak of many ways in which God thwarts those who attempt to do evil and saves the destitute and downtrodden. So rain equalizes, according to Job and this final explanation of the *midrash*, both in raising up the destitute through physical sustenance and in raising those who are low by bringing down those who are powerful and who seek to take advantage of others. "To set on high (*la-marom*) those who are low (*shefalim*)" recalls other biblical (for example, 1 Samuel 2:7) and liturgical passages (such as the blessing after the Shema in the Shaḥarit service) about God raising up those who are low and bringing low those who are high.

Taken together, the *midrash's* first, third, and fourth reasons for rain underscore that rain is something that is beyond human control, that is designed to bring God's blessing equally to everyone, and that operates to equalize the different strata of society. To highlight this ethical understanding of rain, and to introduce a further nuance of "so that all would direct their eyes upward," I want to take note of three brief *midrashim*, each of which relates to a different group of sinners who defied God in the primeval era, after the expulsion from Eden.

The first of these *midrashim* reflects on why the building of the Tower of Babel was such a great sin:

> What did they do?
> Said those of the school of Rabbi Sheila:
> "Let us build a tower, and we will go up to heaven,
> and we will strike it with axes so that its waters will flow."
>
> *Bavli Sanhedrin 109a*

The tower-builders, according to this *midrash*, seek to reach the heavens with a specific purpose in mind—they want to make holes in the firmament so that they can gain access to the water stored in the heavens. In other words, they want to control the flow of water from above. This, according to the talmudic passage, is an unforgivable sin. It is God who controls the rain. According to the first explanation in the Bereishit Rabbah *midrash*, having that control, rather than allowing human beings to have control over water, is the very reason that God decided that the earth would receive its water by means of rain.

The second *midrash* reflects on the notice in Genesis 5:3 that Adam begat his son Seth "in his likeness after his image":

> Rabbi Shimon says:
> From Seth came and were descended
> all of the generations of the righteous,
> and from Cain came and were descended
> all of the generations of the wicked
> who rebel and sin and rebelled against their Rock and said:
> "We do not need the drop of your rains

nor to walk in your ways."
As it says: "And they said to God – Depart from us!"
(Job 21:14).

Pirkei de-Rabbi Eliezer 22

The evil descendants of Cain, according to this *midrash*, reject God's rain. They deny their dependence on God, and they deny their need to follow God's ways. The verse from Job in its entirety reads: "And they said to God – Depart from us! We do not desire knowledge of your ways." Considering the *midrash*'s putting this verse in the mouth of Cain's descendants, we might notice that what the people are rejecting is knowledge—they do not want to *know* God's ways, and they do not want to be dependent on God's gift of rain. In a sense, these descendants of Adam through Cain want to live in an Edenic state, a state in which human beings do not have the knowledge to discern good and evil and do not take responsibility for their choices. They are contrasted with the righteous descendants of Adam through Seth who, the *midrash* implies, accept knowledge and its consequences; they accept their dependence on God's rain, and they accept that they must follow in God's ways.

The Job verse appears as well in the third *midrash*, about the generation of the Flood:

> For they said to God – "Depart from us!
> We do not desire knowledge of your ways.
> Who is the Almighty that we should serve him,
> and what will we gain by praying to him?" (Job 21:14-15).
> They said:
> "Do we need him for anything other than a drop of rain?
> We have rivers and springs from which we are supplied!"
> The Blessed Holy One said:
> "They anger me with the goodness that I bestowed on them—
> and so with that I will sentence them," as it says:
> "And I, behold I am bringing the floodwaters" (Genesis 6:17).

Bavli Sanhedrin 108a

Here, as in the *midrash* about Cain's descendants, the sinners reject God's rain and, with it, knowledge of God's ways and the obligation to serve God. Instead, they believe, they can be supplied with water from rivers and springs, freeing them from dependence on God and the need to follow God's will. This *midrash* is imagining the generation of the Flood as attempting to rewind the biblical story. God shifted from the Edenic *eid* and the rivers that flowed from it to making human beings, post-Eden, dependent on rain. But this generation believes that they can re-capture an Edenic life—the pre-moral universe in which water is simply available without regard to human choice and human behavior. In response, God wields the weapon of rain itself, at once destroying the sinners and asserting that the post-Edenic world is a world in which people are expected to choose between good and evil, a world that is subject to God's judgment expressed in rain.

In each of these *midrashim*, attempting to take control of rain or rejecting dependence on God sending down the rain is an act of rebellion against God and reflects an egregiously evil mindset. In the context of the biblical passages that we have looked at, rejection of God's gift of rain is evil because it is a rejection of God's judgment. It is an attempt to return to a state where water is always available, a state in which human beings are not called to make moral judgments and to act in accordance with what is right. Rejection of rain is the rejection of a consciousness of living in a state of accountability for one's actions. From the perspective of our *midrash* about why God brings rain, rejection of rain or the attempt to regain control of the heavenly waters means rejection of the justice that God seeks to enact by means of giving rain. If rain is designed to thwart the strongmen who would take more than their fair share and to give water to members of society who are weak or poorly-situated, then the tower-builders' and the Cainites' and the Flood generation's rejection of rain is a refusal to share in this ethical vision. They refuse to "direct their eyes upward," to recognize humanity's shared dependence on God.

LOOKING DOWNWARD, LOOKING UPWARD

This points toward another possible understanding of what our *midrash* means when it says that God brings rain "so that all would direct their eyes upward." Here, as we have seen elsewhere in this *midrash*, there seems to be an echo of the Deuteronomy passage about rain. The upward gaze, looking toward the heavens, is the inverse of God's gazing earthward: "It is a land that the Lord your God seeks out; always the eyes of the Lord your God are upon it…" (11:12). In the biblical verse, *God looks downward* to inquire as to how the people are behaving. Are they behaving in accordance with God's will, in which case God will send down rain, or are they violating God's will, which leads to the withholding of rain? In the *midrash*, God decides to make water available through rainfall so that *people will look upward*.

Strikingly, in the Job passage that contains the verse our *midrash* quotes, the verb "to seek" appears, as it does in the Deuteronomy verse. Eliphaz, Job's friend and the speaker in this passage, introduces the verses about rain setting on high those who are low by saying, "But I seek (*edrosh*) unto God" (Job 5:8). The *midrash* seems to pick up on Eliphaz's reference to seeking God in relation to his description of rain, and it reads the sequence of verses in the following way: I seek God, noticing God's gift of rain, which causes people on earth ("those who are low") to set their gaze toward the heavens ("to set on high"). In other words, the *midrash* re-understands what is meant by "to set on high those who are low" by interpreting the phrase in relation to the word "*edrosh.*" As in the Deuteronomy verse God's seeking relates to God's looking earthward, in the Job passage, according to the *midrash*, human seeking relates to human beings' looking heavenward.

But what is it that the *midrash* is suggesting people will see if they look upward in anticipation of rain? Given the *midrash*'s subtle recasting of rain as an instrument of justice, I think the *midrash* is suggesting that, if people look upward toward the source of rain, they will see what rain is all about. They will see—or are being asked to see—that God's purpose for rain is that everyone have an equal share of God's blessing. The *midrash* is saying that rain is designed to create a *consciousness* of how God wants divine blessing to be shared. The reciprocity of the gaze—human beings' looking upward in the *midrash* and God's looking earthward in the biblical verse—suggests a kind of mirroring. People are to mirror God's just gift of rain by sharing their gifts justly. And God mirrors people's just actions, responding in judgment and responding justly, by sending down rain.

Two brief stories in the Talmud Bavli exemplify this mechanism of mirroring. The third chapter of Bavli Ta'anit includes many stories about great sages who, in a time of drought, decree a fast or pray for rain. But, in each case, rain does not come in response to their fasting or prayer. The failure of these rituals to bring rain is particularly striking because the first two chapters of Mishnah Ta'anit are about precisely these two rituals. The first chapter is about series of fast days that are decreed if rain fails to come in its season, and the second chapter is about the special prayer ritual that is performed on those fast days. The stories in the third chapter of Bavli Ta'anit seem designed to undermine any notion we might entertain that we can control the divine gift of rain by means of religious rituals. But in the course of this series of stories, two stories tell of regular people who *do* succeed in bringing rain, in each case after famous sages have failed to do so.

> Rabbi declared a fast, and rain did not come.
> Ilfa—and some say Rabbi Ilfi—
> went down before him [to lead the prayers].
> He said "who causes the wind to blow," and wind blew,
> "who causes the rain to fall," and rain came.
> He [Rabbi] said to him: "What do you do?"
> He said to him: "I live in a poor village
> where there is no wine for Kiddush and Havdallah.
> I toil to bring wine for Kiddush and Havdallah
> and help them fulfill their obligation."
>
> Rav went to a certain place.
> He declared a fast, and rain did not come.
> The prayer leader went down before him.
> He said "who causes the wind to blow," and wind blew,
> "who causes the rain to fall," and rain came.
> He [Rav] said to him: "What do you do?"
> He said to him: "I am a teacher of young children,
> and I teach the children of the poor like the children of the rich,
> and whoever is unable [to pay] I do not take anything from him.
> And I have a fish pond—
> and anyone who does wrong, I bribe him with them
> and I arrange things for him
> and I appease him until he comes and reads."
>
> *Bavli Ta'anit 24a*

In each of these stories, the person who succeeds in praying for rain is someone who shares equally among everyone the blessing that they have to offer. The schoolteacher does not distinguish between rich and poor, between those who can pay his fee and those who cannot. Similarly, he makes whatever effort it takes to teach each child to read, no matter what difficulties the child might have that hold him back. The first prayer leader enables each person in his town to fulfill their ritual obligations. He toils to bring the wine that they need but cannot afford.

What is remarkable about these two stories is not just that these ordinary individuals succeed in bringing rain after prominent sages have failed. What is less obvious, but crucial for understanding these stories, is that the two prayer leaders do not even offer the special prayers for a fast day, prescribed in the second chapter of Mishnah Ta'anit, which insert special blessings into the Amidah that plead for God to help in a time of crisis. In fact, the two prayer leaders do not ask for anything at all. They have not even uttered the request for rain that is a part of the middle section of the regular daily Amidah, the prayer that is described in the first chapter of Mishnah Ta'anit with the expression *sho'alin et ha-geshamim*—asking for rain (1:2). They never get that far. The rain begins to fall when the prayers are merely up to the second blessing of the Amidah, the blessing that describes God's powers, into which, during the rainy season, mention of God's power to bring rain is inserted—what is described in the first chapter of Mishnah Ta'anit as *mazkirin gevurot geshamim*—mentioning the power of rain (1:1). God hears each of these individuals saying, "You are the one who sends down the rain," and God sends down the rain. So what is it that enables the mere mention of God's rain-giving power to trigger this divine gift?

I believe that what is at play here is the mechanism of mirroring—the midrashic human gaze heavenward mirroring the biblical divine gaze downward. God looks down from the heavens to see whether people fulfill God's will. Human beings look upward to understand God's will as manifest in rain, God's wish that blessings be available equally to all. In these two stories, the individuals who pray are people who enact that divine vision, working hard to ensure that all of the people with whom they interact have equal access to the gifts that they have to offer. They have mirrored the justice of God's heavenly blessing, and so God is called to mirror the justice of those who work on the earth. These individuals' simple mention of God as the one who sends down rain calls God to shower down the blessing that is meant to be shared and that human beings are working to share.

"WHO SENDS FORTH HIS WORD TO THE LAND"

The *midrash* with which we began asks us to notice the way in which the world receives its water. It points us toward biblical texts that suggest that rain is an innovation that God introduces, not an element of the world as it was first created. Rain, according to these biblical texts, is an instrument of judgment, a mechanism that God deploys in the post-Edenic world in which human beings are expected to make moral choices and are held accountable for those choices.

Drawing on the biblical idea of rain as an instrument of judgment, the *midrash* subtly transforms rain into an instrument of *justice*. Rain is a medium of equalizing access to God's gifts, so that strong and weak, rich and poor share in those gifts and, as well, recognize their shared dependence on God. This recognition, as midrashic stories about sinners who *rejected* God's gift of rain illustrate, is not only an acceptance of dependency and vulnerability. It is an acceptance of accountability, of the obligation that comes with Adam and Eve's eating of the fruit of the Tree of Knowledge and their expulsion from Eden into a world watered by rain. Human beings now have the power of moral discernment and the opportunity afforded by rain to discern God's ways and to shape their behavior in accordance with God's will.

The midrashic idea that rain causes people to "direct their eyes upward," we saw, parallels Deuteronomy's image of God looking downward toward the promised land and its people to determine whether rain should fall or be withheld. This reciprocal gaze suggests a kind of mirroring, in which people look upward to understand and emulate the just way in which God shares God's gifts, and God looks downward, judging human action and responding justly. The talmudic stories about individuals who succeed in praying for rain—or rather, in prompting God to give rain without even asking for it—exemplify this very mirroring. Each of these individuals has manifested God's will as expressed in the gift of rain, and God responds by showering down the blessing of rain.

These biblical and rabbinic texts about rain invite us to imagine rain as a form of revelation. Rain is a bridge between heaven and earth, a physical manifestation of God's involvement in the world, a non-verbal divine message. The Psalmist celebrates God's giving of rain: "Who covers the heavens with clouds, provides rain for the land, makes mountains put forth grass" and continues, "who sends forth his word to the land, his command runs swiftly" (Psalm 147:8, 15). One way to understand this second verse is to see rain as following God's command; thus, the fulfillment of God's will is evident in the world. But another way to understand the psalm is that rain is *itself* God's word. God's command, then, is not manifest in rain simply because rain obeys God's command. Rather, God's command is manifest in rain because rain *is* God's commanding message. It is the way in which God communicates to us God's will for how the world is to be run, by God as well as by God's human creations.

The texts we have looked at urge us to experience rain as the word that, in the words of the Psalmist, God sends forth to earth. They invite us to experience rain not simply as a natural phenomenon but as something that evokes a consciousness of God's care, God's demand, God's judgment, and God's justice. They remind us that, having left Eden, we have no choice but to exercise moral discernment and to take moral actions. We do not live in a world watered by an *eid*; we live in a world watered by rain. And, to guide us in our choices, rain invites us to look heavenward and to shape our actions in this fallen world on the model of the divine gift of rain.

DARKNESS WILL ENVELOP ME

Rav said:
Kalends was established
by the first human being (*adam ha-rishon*).
When he saw that the night was getting longer,
he said:
"Woe to me lest the one about whom it is written:
'He shall wound (*yeshufkha*) your head
and you shall wound (*teshufenu*) his heel' (Genesis 3:15)
will come to bite me."
"And I said:
'Surely darkness will envelop me (*yeshufeini*)' (Psalm 139:11)."
When he saw that the day was getting longer,
he said: "*Kalends!*"—*kalon dio*.

Yerushalmi Avodah Zarah 1:2/39c

THIS BRIEF STORY in the Talmud Yerushalmi tells of the terror of Adam when, shortly after coming into being, he notices that the days are changing. Adam, according to this tradition, was created in the fall. He begins to see that each day brings a longer and longer night. Never having experienced the seasons before and having no source of knowledge other than his own experience, Adam thinks that this pattern will continue and that the nights will keep getting longer and longer, the daytime shorter and shorter. He is terrified.

What is it that makes Adam feel so vulnerable? The passage gives us an insight into Adam's terror by calling our attention to a word that appears in two verses, one from the story of Adam in Genesis and the other from Psalm 139. This psalm is commonly understood in rabbinic tradition as reflecting the experience of Adam. In the verse from the psalm that is quoted here, the speaker talks about his own experience, reflecting on something that he had thought: "And I said: 'Surely darkness will envelop me.'" The word that I have translated as "envelop" is *yeshufeini*, the same verb that is used in Genesis to describe the state of enmity that God told Adam, in the aftermath of Adam's sin, will exist between Adam and the snake: "He shall wound (*yeshufkha*) your head and you shall wound (*teshufenu*) his heel." The Yerushalmi passage takes the words of the psalm, understood as Adam's own words, and re-understands them in relation to the Genesis verse. While the plain meaning of the Psalms verse is something like "Surely darkness will envelop me," darkness serving as the subject of the verb *yeshufeini*, the talmudic story reads "Surely in darkness *he* will wound me." *He* is the snake.

Adam's world is no longer a safe place. In the aftermath of his sin, Adam feels vulnerable. God has told Adam that he will be in unmitigated conflict with the snake, and darkness, Adam fears, gives the snake an opportunity to attack him. As the nights get increasingly longer, a greater part of each day leaves Adam vulnerable to that which he most fears.

Returning to the Psalms verse that, in our passage, articulates Adam's fear, I think that its plain meaning and the midrashic understanding are not so far apart. The midrashic reading gives voice to a very particular fear, fear of the snake, but we might understand this more broadly as a very primal fear, not so different from anyone's fear of the dark. Darkness envelops us, and we feel vulnerable to whatever it is that most terrifies us: ghosts, monsters, our own thoughts, our nightmares, our inadequacies, our mortality, our guilt. Adam's fear of the snake, similarly, can be understood as the terror that grips him in the aftermath of his sin. He has failed, he has been cast out of Eden, he has been pronounced mortal – and the world is getting darker and darker.

Rabbinic tradition's understanding of Psalm 139 as telling specifically of Adam's experience can be seen as a narrowing of the subject of the psalm to the experience of a single, specific person at a particular moment in time. But, alternatively, it can be seen as a broadening of the experiences that the psalm describes. *Adam ha-rishon* is both Adam, the first human individual about whom the Torah tells a story, and all humankind. Reading the psalm as a window into Adam's experiences is an invitation to each of us to imagine ourselves in the words of the psalm. Each of us experiences times in which we are plunged into darkness, times in which the world is getting darker and darker around us. Each of us knows the terror of those moments in which we do not know that the darkness will ever give way to the light.

> And I said: "Surely darkness will envelop me,
> and the light shall be night about me."

The second part of the Psalms verse that describes the experience of being enveloped by darkness can be read in two different ways, each of which is attested in contemporary biblical translations. The first reading, which is reflected in the translation above, takes the second part of the verse as reiterating the first part or taking it a step further. The speaker is saying that, even in times of light, he is shrouded in darkness. Reading the verse as spoken by Adam, the verse tells of the days leading to the winter solstice. Not only is Adam vulnerable when it is dark, but even *light*—that is, even what until now has been daytime—is becoming *night*. And, as far as Adam knows, this process will continue until there is only nighttime and no more light, until he will be totally enveloped by darkness.

But, because the words "night" and "light" are not linked by a verb in the Hebrew text, and because the biblical text leaves ambiguous which word should be understood as the grammatical subject, the second part of the verse can be read in the opposite way: *the night has become light for me*. According to this reading, what the speaker recalls having said or thought constitutes only the first part of the verse. The second part articulates what actually happened, in contrast to what the speaker had anticipated and feared. And so the conjunction that links the two halves of the verses would be translated as *but* rather than *and*:

> And I said: "Surely darkness will envelop me,"
> but the night has become light for me.

Reading this verse as spoken by Adam, Adam is reflecting on how he had *thought* that he would be enveloped by darkness. But the days pass and the solstice comes, and gradually the daylight hours begin to increase. Adam had thought that darkness would take over, but what had been *nighttime*, he sees, is now becoming *light*.

35

The second part of this verse, then, can be read to express both of Adam's experiences, his experience of day turning into night and his experience of night turning into day. It describes both the terrifying experience of feeling vulnerable to what he imagines will be the ever-increasing darkness, and also the feeling of relief as darkness begins to give way to light. Rereading the verse with *both* of these possibilities in mind—taking the verse's ambiguity not as something to be resolved but as expressing its complex meaning—allows us simultaneously to experience the deep terror of the darkness and the relief and joy of anticipation of light's return. Both of these, the story tells us, were foundational experiences of the first human being, and both of these are experiences of every human being.

The story in the Yerushalmi about Adam's first winter folds within it the story of Adam's sin and punishment in Genesis, and the experience of human vulnerability and redemption described in the psalm. Bringing these two biblical texts into conversation with each other and with the story that it tells, the Yerushalmi crafts a narrative characterized by both simplicity and depth. The Bavli tells a similar story about Adam and adds an additional layer of complexity by bringing another talmudic text into conversation with the story that it tells. This text is not cited explicitly in the Bavli story about Adam but is evoked through language and motifs that it shares with this story. We will turn to this text after considering the Bavli story and comparing it with the parallel story in the Yerushalmi.

BEHIND AND BEFORE

Both the Bavli and Yerushalmi stories appear in relation to a *mishnah* that lists pagan festivals:

> These are the festivals of the idolaters:
> Kalends and Saturnalia....
>
> *Mishnah Avodah Zarah* 1:3

The Yerushalmi story is offered as an explanation of the origin of the holiday of Kalends. Rav explains that Kalends originated with Adam. When Adam saw the day getting longer, he exclaimed "*Kalends!*" Adam's exclamation, which generates the name of the holiday, is etymologized by the Yerushalmi as deriving from "*kalon dio.*" "*Kalon*" is Greek for beautiful or good. "*Dio*" is explained in different ways by the commentaries (see the alternatives in the commentary of the Penei Moshe): either as the Greek or Latin for God or as the Latin for day. Thus, Adam is either praising God for bringing light out of the darkness, or celebrating the lengthening of the day after the solstice.

The Bavli tells a similar story in explanation of the origin of both Kalends and Saturnalia. But first it identifies the dates of these two holidays and offers a mnemonic for remembering the order of the holidays:

> Rav Ḥanan bar Rava said:
> Kalends—eight days following the solstice.
> Saturnalia—eight days preceding the solstice.
> And your mnemonic:
> "You have beset me behind and before etc." (Psalm 139:5).
>
> Our Rabbis taught:
> When the first human being (*adam ha-rishon*)
> saw the day getting shorter and shorter,
> he said:
> "Woe to me,
> perhaps because I have sinned, the world is dark about me
> and is returning to chaos and confusion,
> and this is the death
> that has been sentenced upon me from the heavens."
> He sat for eight days in fasting.
> When he saw the winter solstice
> and saw the day getting longer and longer,
> he said:
> "This is the way of the world."
> He went and made eight festive days.
> Another year he made these and these into festive days.
> He established them for the sake of heaven,
> but they established them for the sake of idolatry.
>
> *Bavli Avodah Zarah 8a*

Rav Ḥanan bar Rava explains that the first holiday listed in the *mishnah*, Kalends, takes place eight days *after* the solstice, and the second holiday,

Saturnalia, takes place eight days *before* the solstice. This means that the holidays are listed in reverse order in the *mishnah*, a fact that suggests the need for the mnemonic that follows.

In the verse that is quoted as the aid to memory, the word "behind" (*aḥor*) precedes the word "before" (*kedem*). In rabbinic texts, "behind" refers to what is in the future. For example, in the famous story of Moses visiting the *beit midrash* of Rabbi Akiva, God says to Moses "turn behind you" (*ḥazor le-aḥorekha*), and Moses is then able to step into the future (Bavli Menaḥot 29b). Conversely, what is in the past is that which is before or in front of a person. This directionality is counterintuitive to us, who see the past as behind us, and who imagine ourselves as oriented toward the future, which lies before or ahead of us. But in rabbinic imagination, one faces what has already happened; this is what can be known and this is how we orient ourselves. The future is what we cannot see; it is in the back of us. And so the mnemonic is saying that what is behind—that is, what is in the future, what will come later—precedes what is before—that is, what is in the past, what comes earlier. Thus, with this verse in mind, we can remember that the *mishnah* lists the *later* holiday, Kalends, before the *earlier* holiday, Saturnalia.

But why this oblique mnemonic? Why would it be likely that one would remember this verse and its implication for the order of the holidays listed in the *mishnah*? The use of this mnemonic only makes sense if we recognize that the verse is from Psalm 139, the psalm that is understood as telling about Adam's experiences and that is quoted explicitly in the Yerushalmi version of the story of Adam and the increasing darkness. The Bavli story about Adam does not explicitly quote the psalm, but the appearance of a verse from Psalm 139 at this point sets a backdrop for the story that immediately follows, bringing the psalm and the experiences of which it tells into our consciousness as we set about reading the story.

This particular verse—offered here as a reminder of the holidays that Adam established—is interpreted elsewhere in the Bavli as articulating Adam's experience of diminution after his sin (Ḥagigah 12a). Adam, according to Rabbi Elazar, was gigantic at creation; he reached from the earth to the heavens. But after Adam sinned (*saraḥ*), God placed God's hand on him and diminished him. Rav Yehudah transmits a similar tradition in the name of Rav: At creation, Adam stretched from one end of the earth to the other; when he sinned, he was diminished under God's hand. Both derive the idea of Adam's diminution from the Psalms verse:

"You have beset me behind and before, and you placed your hand upon me" (139:5).

The word translated here as "beset me"—*tzartani*—has also been understood as "formed," recalling the creation of the human being: "The Lord God formed (*va-yitzer*) the human being from the dust of the earth" (Genesis 2:7). Rashi explains the talmudic interpretation of the verse that tells of Adam's diminution as based on this latter understanding of the word *tzartani*: "You have formed me behind and before" refers to two separate acts of creation, an earlier one in which Adam is gigantic, and a later one in which he is small—or, in Rashi's words, creations in which Adam is high and then low (Rashi on Ḥagigah 12a). Alternatively, the talmudic sages might be interpreting the entire first part of the verse as referring to Adam's initial creation, the words "behind and before" suggesting that he stretched from one extreme point to the other (from earth to heaven or from one end of the earth to the other), and only the second half of the verse—"and you placed your hand upon me"—as referring to Adam's diminution after his sin.

Another possibility is that the sages are reading the word *tzartani* in both ways simultaneously, as conveying the meaning both of formation and of constricting (perhaps construing *tzartani* as relating to the word *tzar*, "narrow"—"you narrowed me"). The human being, according to this reading, is a creature whose essence is both of vast capacity and of extreme limitation. Adam both can reach from earth to heaven—or from one end of the earth to the other—and can be so very small. Such a reading fits with the reading I offered above of the verse about light and darkness. There, too, the verse can be construed in two ways, and I suggested that the talmudic story includes both of these readings and, indeed, invites us to imagine both meanings simultaneously.

This bivalence can be read as central to Psalm 139's meaning and purpose. The human being in this psalm is portrayed as worthy of God's notice and, at the same time, as fragile and vulnerable in relation to God. The speaker talks about the impossibility of escaping from God's presence, in verses that can be read both as suggesting an attempt to flee from God and as conveying the awesome assurance of finding God everywhere. The paradoxical nature of the psalm's portrayal of the human condition, and especially of the human experience of being in God's presence, is captured and highlighted in Israel Najara's liturgical poem based on this psalm, *Anah Eileikh*. The poem begins by quoting Psalm 139:7—*anah eileikh mei-ruḥekha anah mi-panekha evraḥ*, "Where can I go from your spirit? Where can I flee from your presence?"—and continues: *evraḥ mimkha eilekha*—"I flee *from* you *to* you."

This very duality might lie at the heart of the rabbinic attribution of the psalm to Adam, the human being formed from the dust of the ground but ensouled with God's spirit (Genesis 2:7), the person who lives in a place in which God walks, and who tries to hide from the presence of God, only to find that his hiding, and perhaps the very place in which he hides, reveals to God his thoughts and actions (3:8-11).

The talmudic understanding of the verse that the Bavli introduces as a mnemonic just before the story about Adam and the increasing darkness captures this duality. The verse evokes the midrashic idea that Adam had once filled the entire earth, but Adam sinned and was diminished. It is worth noting that the word used for "sin" in the talmudic passage about Adam's diminution is *saraḥ*, the same word that is used in the story about Adam establishing the festivals for which the Psalms verse is cited as a mnemonic: "perhaps because I have sinned (*saraḥti*)...." Citing this verse as the story of Adam and the darkness is about to begin brings to mind the complex experience of the human being described in the psalm and, in particular, the notion of Adam sinning and what happens to Adam as a consequence of his sin.

THE WAY OF THE WORLD

The Bavli story is very similar to the Yerushalmi story, but there are a few notable differences. In the Yerushalmi story, Adam is worried that the snake will come and attack him in the darkness. In the Bavli, it is darkness itself that terrifies Adam. Adam's words "the world is dark about me (*ba'adi*)" recalls the Psalms verse about light and darkness: "And I said: 'Surely darkness will envelop me, and the light shall be night about me (*ba'adeini*).'" Adam is saying that the world is dark *about himself*—meaning not only that it is dark *for* him but also, perhaps, that the world is dark *because* of him.

Adam imagines that, because he has sinned, darkness has come to the world. And he believes that this darkness, overtaking the world more and more each day, signals that the world is returning to primordial chaos. The first act of creation in Genesis is the creation of light (Genesis 1:3). Before that, "the earth was unformed and void (*tohu va-vohu*) and darkness was upon the face of the deep" (1:2). If the earth is returning to darkness, then it is returning to *tohu va-vohu*—the very words that Adam uses in our story. Adam has caused the dissolution of creation, the return of the world to its pre-creation state of darkness and chaos. This, he believes, is the death that he had been warned about should he fail to obey God's word (2:17).

In the waning days of winter, the newly created Adam imagines the world as an extension of himself; the death to which he had been condemned is the extinction of the world. His own offense—*saraḥti* evokes decay or rot—returns the world to chaos and confusion. But at the solstice, there is a shift in Adam's consciousness. When Adam sees the days getting longer and longer, he says: "This is the way of the world."

It is not clear what causes this change in the way Adam sees the world. Why does he not believe, instead, that God has responded to his fasting, that God has forgiven him and halted the process set in motion by his sin? Perhaps Adam's new understanding comes about because he sees the daylight increasing gradually; if God had forgiven him and halted the world's return to darkness, the lengthening nights would be expected simply to stop lengthening, or perhaps suddenly to return to their pre-sin duration. Instead, Adam notices a gradual shift in the length of daytime, and that does not seem to him to be a response to his fasting. Rather, he concludes, this—both the lengthening of daytime that he experiences now and, in retrospect, the lengthening of nighttime that he experienced earlier—is the way of the world.

Adam now is alienated from his world. He understands the world to be separate from himself; it is not affected by his actions or his state of being. The increasing light is not a function of his fasting, and the decreasing light was not a function of his sin. Thus, he not only celebrates the time of increasing light, but he subsequently turns the earlier days into festive days as well. The world will continue as it is, with longer and longer nights giving way to longer and longer days. This realization, the story tells us, is the origin of the two eight-day festivals of Kalends and Saturnalia.

FESTIVE DAYS

Eight-day festivals?

In the introduction to our passage in the Bavli, Rav Ḥanan bar Rava dates Kalends to eight days after the solstice and Saturnalia to eight days before. This corresponds to the dates on which these holidays in fact fell on the Roman calendar. Saturnalia was held on December 17th, eight days before the winter solstice, which, on the Julian calendar, fell on December 25th. Kalends was a first-of-the-month festival, so the Kalends of January fell eight days after the December 25th solstice.

But Rav Ḥanan bar Rava is not necessarily suggesting that these holidays are eight days long. That is a subtle change introduced in the story about Adam's establishment of these festivals, and it does not correspond to the actual Roman holidays. In fact, Kalends was a one-day festival, and Saturnalia varied in duration from one to seven days during different periods. Neither was an eight-day long festival. According to the story about Adam, though, Saturnalia began on December 17th and continued, *for eight days*, through the 24th, and Kalends began on December 25th and continued, *for eight days*, through January 1st.

So why does this story tell of Adam's celebration of eight-day holidays? I believe that this story was shaped in the Bavli in relation to the practice of lighting Hanukkah candles and to the Hanukkah story. Here is the Bavli's discussion of how to light the Hanukkah candles, followed by the story of Hanukkah's origins:

> Our Rabbis taught:
> The *mitzvah* of Hanukkah
> is a candle for each person and his household;
> and those who beautify—a candle for each and every one;
> and those who most beautify—
> Beit Shammai say:
> The first day he lights eight;
> from then on he lessens and lessens,
> and Beit Hillel say:
> The first night he lights one;
> from then on he increases and increases. ...

What is Hanukkah?
As our Rabbis taught:
On the 25th of Kislev are the eight days of Hanukkah,
not to eulogize on them and not to fast on them.
For when the Greeks entered the Temple,
they defiled all of the oil in the Temple.
And when the Hasmonean dynasty
prevailed and defeated them,
they searched and found only one cruse of oil
that lay with the seal of the High Priest,
and there was only enough in it to light for one day.
A miracle was done with it, and they lit from it for eight days.
Another year they established them
and made them into festive days with praise and thanksgiving.

Bavli Shabbat 21b

This description of the origins of Hanukkah shares several details with the Bavli's story about Adam and the winter solstice. Hanukkah, of course, is an eight-day holiday, like Kalends and Saturnalia according to the Bavli's story about the origin of these festivals. It falls on the 25th day of the month of Kislev, a date similar to the pivot point of the two festivals that Adam is said to have established, one beginning eight days before the December 25th solstice and the other beginning on the December 25th solstice.

After each of the stories describes the way the holidays originated, both conclude by saying that, at a later time (*le-shanah aheret*) there was a change. Originally, Adam fasted during the first eight days and celebrated the second eight days as festive days (*yamim tovim*). But, "another year," he made both of them into festive days. The original eight days of Hanukkah were days in which the miracle of the oil unfolded. But "another year," they established these as festive days, on which fasting is forbidden. Both stories use the word *kava*—"established"—in describing how the holidays reached their final form. Adam "established" the holidays for the sake of heaven, but others "established" them for the sake of idolatry. Hanukkah was "established" and made into festive days with praise and thanksgiving.

Finally, both passages talk about decreasing light and increasing light. In the Adam story, the day is *mitma'eit ve-holeikh*—it gets shorter and shorter—and then it is *ma'arikh ve-holeikh*—it gets longer and longer. In the Hanukkah passage, Beit Shammai and Beit Hillel dispute how the candles ought to be lit. According to Beit Shammai, on the first day one lights eight candles and, from then on, *poḥeit ve-holeikh*—one lessens and lessens; that is, one lights fewer and fewer candles each day. According to Beit Hillel, on the first day one lights one candle and, from then on, *mosif ve-holeikh*—one increases and increases; that is, one lights more and more candles each day.

These similarities, both in content and in formulation, suggest that the two passages are shaped in relation to each other. Note that the Yerushalmi version of the Adam story contains not a single one of the elements listed above that are shared between the Bavli version of that story and the passage about Hanukkah. The story about Adam in the Bavli seems to be deliberately shaped to echo elements of the Hanukkah passage, and it is possible that the Hanukkah passage itself was partially shaped in relation to the Adam passage. Thus, the Bavli is inviting us to hear the story of Adam when we read the Hanukkah story, and to keep the Hanukkah story in mind when we read the story of Adam. This interplay between texts creates a dynamic space into which the reader is invited to enter and find meaning.

ADAM AND HANUKKAH

The Adam story broadens the significance of the Hanukkah story. While Hanukkah marks a particular event in Jewish history, the Adam story invites us to understand Hanukkah as celebrating a universal human experience as well. Adam—the first human being and every human being—experiences the terror of being engulfed by the darkness. And Adam experiences the return of the light after a period of darkness that threatens never to end. Hanukkah, understood in relation to the story of Adam, becomes a holiday in which a one-time victory over tyrants, rededication of the Temple, and lighting the tiny remnant of oil signify as well an event of ongoing significance in each individual life and in the universal experience of humankind.

The Adam story also helps us notice that Hanukkah is a holiday about both increasing light and decreasing light. Beit Shammai's and Beit Hillel's positions are alternatives *in practice*, but the two ways of lighting the candles coexist in our text—within the talmudic passage, we are offered both an image of diminishing light and an image of increasing light. In fact, Hanukkah falls at the very darkest time of the year. With respect to the solar calendar, Hanukkah falls not far from the winter solstice, when the nights are longest. With respect to the lunar calendar, Hanukkah begins shortly before new moon, when the last sliver of the waning moon is about to disappear. An eight-day holiday that begins on the 25th of a lunar month takes us through a period of disappearing light into a time of greatest darkness and then into a time in which the light begins to reappear, with the emergence of the waxing moon.

Hanukkah, then, mirrors Adam's experience of diminishing and growing light, but does so specifically on the Jewish lunar-solar calendar. Beit Shammai's and Beit Hillel's positions about how to light the Hanukkah candles—formulated, as we saw, in language that echoes the Adam story—mirror Adam's experience as well. Instead of eight days of decreasing light followed by eight days of increasing light generating two consecutive festivals, as in the Adam story, Hanukkah is a single festival of eight days in which—within our textual tradition—the light of the candles simultaneously both decreases and increases. It is as if the Hanukkah passage folds the two parts of Adam's experience over onto one another, asking us to experience the decreasing light and the increasing light at one and the same time. This complicates the experience of darkness, suggesting, perhaps, that not only will darkness inevitably give way to the light—as in the Adam story—but that darkness and light are interwoven in some way. Perhaps we are invited to imagine ways in which the experience of darkness itself might—at least from the perspective of *another year*—be a source of light.

Finally, the Adam story traces Adam's maturation from having a consciousness of the world as an extension of himself, to having a consciousness that is alienated from the world. At the story's end, Adam believes that "this is the way of the world," and that his behavior and his state of being have no impact on the way the world is. The story of Hanukkah asks us to reevaluate this vision of our place in the world. Like Adam, we live in a world that has an existence independent of ourselves. But Adam celebrates the way the world is with praise and thanksgiving, having concluded that the world is not changed by his own actions. On Hanukkah, in contrast, we offer praise and thanksgiving for the miracle of the oil, reminding ourselves of the possibility of finding and creating sources of light in a very dark time, and celebrating by lighting candles each year in the time of greatest darkness. The passage about Hanukkah, read in relation to the story about Adam, invites us to imagine how a human being who accepts the realization to which Adam comes can nevertheless believe in our ability to affect the world.

The dispute between Beit Hillel and Beit Shammai has always puzzled me. I suggested above that the two positions side-by-side offer a generative experience of overlapping increasing and diminishing light. But, as *alternative* positions about how to light the candles, Beit Hillel's position, the one that is universally followed, seems quite sensible, and Beit Shammai's position seems almost incomprehensible. Why would we think to have a candle-lighting practice that moves from eight candles down to one, that has us celebrate Hanukkah by creating an experience of diminishing light?

But perhaps we can understand Beit Shammai's position in light of the notion that Hanukkah moves us from a stance of alienation from the world to a belief in the possibility of having an impact on the world. Beit Hillel's position has us reflecting the light that is about to increase, or perhaps modeling the increase that we anticipate we will soon experience. But Beit Shammai asks us to do something different. Beit Shammai asks us, in the very darkest time, when the last sliver of light is about to disappear, to put a blast of light into the world. Our actions light up the world and, over time, as the world begins to brighten, we need to put in less and less light. Beit Hillel, in other words, has us lighting the candles as a form of *pirsumei nisa*—publicizing the miracle—responding to or anticipating the change from darkness to light by reflecting that change, increasing the light of the candles from night to night. In a sense, we are like Adam, responding to the change that we experience with praise and thanksgiving. But Beit Shammai does not have us *responding* to the change. Beit Shammai asks us to *create* that change, to enter into the experience of being plunged into darkness and to give out all of the light that we can muster.

Alternatively, perhaps both Beit Shammai and Beit Hillel understand lighting the Hanukkah candles as expressing our ability to bring light to the world, rather than as a reflection of the world becoming brighter. Perhaps their *mahloket*—their conflicting positions—reflect different understandings of how we can make change. Beit Shammai believes that in the darkest time we need to oppose the darkness with all of our energy and resources – we need to *fight* the darkness with a blast of light. Beit

Hillel offers a different approach, starting as small as we find ourselves able to do, adding just a tiny bit of light, and creating the possibility of doing a bit more each day.

The echo between the Hanukkah passage and the story of Adam—and the psalm that both versions of the Adam story evoke—opens dimensions of imaginative experiences of Hanukkah that go beyond the familiar story of Hanukkah that the Bavli explicitly relates. Within this intertextual space, Hanukkah becomes a time that allows us to mark the experience of darkness, the terror and uncertainty that each person faces at times when light, literally or figuratively, seems to be slipping away – as it did for the first human being and as it does, at times, for each of us. It becomes a holiday in which we search for tiny points of light, a holiday that promises us that small sources of light *can* be found and that, no matter how dark it is, light will return to the world again. The eight days of Hanukkah and the candle-lighting practices that the Talmud describes evoke an overlapping of decreasing and increasing light, offering an experience of darkness and light that are interwoven with each other, as they are in the verse from Psalms that the Yerushalmi imagines Adam speaking, and as they so often are even in our most difficult and our most joyful life events. And the *mitzvah* of candle-lighting holds out the promise that, even though, as children of Adam, we are very small, each one of us does have the capacity—and so the responsibility—to bring some light into a world that can be very dark.

WORK AND ITS PURPOSES

That is why they are crying out saying:
"Let us go sacrifice to our God."
Let the labor be heavier upon the men,
and let them do it (*ya'asu*),
so that they not pay attention (*yish'u*) to deceitful words.

Exodus 5:8-9

This teaches that they possessed scrolls
in which they would delight (*mishta'ash'in*)
from Shabbat to Shabbat,
saying that the Blessed Holy One will redeem them,
because they would rest on Shabbat.
Pharaoh said to them:
"'Let the labor be heavier upon the men,
and let them do it (*ya'asu*),
so that they not pay attention (*yish'u*) ...'—
let them not delight (*mishta'ash'in*)
and let them not be refreshed on the Shabbat day."

Shemot Rabbah 5:18

THE STORY OF Israel's becoming a nation is framed by acts of labor. The book of Exodus begins with the Israelites' building project for Pharaoh and culminates with their building project for God. Servitude and service are enacted through labor, and the book allows us to trace what it means to be a slave and what it means to be free by telling about the kinds of work that are performed by the Israelites as they journey from enslavement to freedom. The stories with which the book begins and ends, as well as the story in which the newly-freed Israelites work to gather the manna, invite us to consider the nature of each kind of work, its goals, and the conception of individual and community that it embodies and fosters.

Pharaoh first enslaves the Israelites in the very first chapter of Exodus, but the richest description of his methods and purposes appears in the episode about the manufacture of bricks in chapter 5. Moses and Aaron have just gone on their first mission to Pharaoh, bringing God's message: "Send my people that they may hold a feast to me in the wilderness" (Exodus 5:1). Pharaoh, of course, refuses; he declares that he does not know Y-H-V-H and will not listen to Y-H-V-H's voice (5:2). He accuses Moses and Aaron of distracting the people from their work (*tafri'u*, a play on the name "Pharaoh") and worries that the people will cease from their burdensome labor (5:4-5).

In reaction, Pharaoh commands that the Israelites no longer be given the raw material with which to manufacture bricks. From now on, they will have to go and gather their own straw. Nevertheless, they will be held accountable to produce the same quantity of bricks as they were able to manufacture before. This plan, Pharaoh anticipates, will keep the people from turning to false hopes of going to worship their God (5:6-9).

This episode discloses Pharaoh's goals in imposing labor on the people. Pharaoh is not a king who wants to build cities and monuments and who enslaves a people in order to get an army of laborers to do the work. If that were the case, then the most effective method of getting the work done would be to provide all of the materials that the laborers need. But it has been clear since chapter 1, when Pharaoh first set the Israelites to building, that Pharaoh's main interest is not getting his building projects accomplished. Pharaoh worried about Israel becoming a large and mighty nation, and so he decided "to oppress them with burdensome labor; and they built store-cities for Pharaoh: Pithom and Ramses" (1:9-11). The purpose of the labor was not to create store-cities; the store-cities were a by-product of the labor, the purpose of which was to oppress the Israelites.

And so, in chapter 5, when Pharaoh sees that the labor is not difficult enough to achieve his goals of oppression, Pharaoh makes the work harder, ensuring that the people will not be able to meet the daily goal set for them. When the Israelite overseers are beaten by the Egyptian taskmasters because of the slaves' inevitable failure to meet their quota of brick production, they complain to Pharaoh about the new policy, and Pharaoh reiterates his goal: "Idle, you are idle! That is why you say 'Let us go worship Y-H-V-H.' And now, go and labor..." (5:17-18). Pharaoh wants to make sure that the Israelites have no cessation from labor, no space in which to think about anything other than the work that they have been set to accomplish. They are not to think about where they want to "go"; they are to "go" and do their work, laboriously and unceasingly.

Work in this story, then, is not goal-directed; the fruits of the labor are not the purpose of the labor. By saying that those who want to go worship the Lord are to go work for Pharaoh instead, by denying knowledge of God in refusing to allow the people to go to worship God, Pharaoh is setting *himself* up as a kind of god. He has complete control over the people, all of whose thoughts and energies and time are to be consumed with serving his will.

EGYPT, EDEN, AND BABEL

Pharaoh introduces his new plan to keep the Israelites in their place with the words *hein* and *atah* ("behold" and "now"): "*Behold*, the people of the land *now* are many..." (Exodus 5:5). This pair of words appears twice in the early narratives of the book of Genesis. The first occurrence is at the end of the Garden of Eden story: "The Lord God said: '*Behold*, the human being has become like one of us, knowing good and evil, and *now* lest (*pen*) he put forth his hand and take also from the Tree of Life and eat and live forever'" (Genesis 3:22). God is concerned about the human being breaching the boundaries between the human and the divine, and so God decides to banish the human being from the Garden, setting up a barrier between the human being and the Tree of Life and thus limiting the human being's capacity to be godlike.

The second occurrence of this pair of words is in the Tower of Babel story. The people who have gathered in the plain of Shinar devise a plan to build a city with a tower whose top will reach the heavens (11:4). God comes down to see what the people (literally, "the children of *ha-adam*— the human being") have built and says: "*Behold*, they are one people and there is one language for all of them, and this is what they have begun to do, and *now* nothing that they plot to do will be withheld from them" (11:5-6). In response, God confuses their language and scatters the people across the land so that they stop building the city (11:7-8).

Both of these stories are about limits: God acts to set limits on what human beings can do out of concern to establish a boundary between human beings and God. The human being cannot have both knowledge and immortality, and human beings cannot join together with the purpose of reaching the heavens. That Pharaoh's words echo God's expression of concern that human beings might breach the boundary that separates the human and the divine underscores the idea that Pharaoh is setting himself up as a god, establishing himself as the figure who has the right and the power to diminish the aspirations and activities of his human subjects.

The launching of Pharaoh's plan of oppression at the very beginning of the enslavement narrative also includes words that appear in the Garden of Eden and Tower of Babel stories: *"Behold (hineih)*, the nation of the Children of Israel is too many and mighty for us. *Come (havah)*, let us deal wisely with them, *lest (pen)* they multiply..." (Exodus 1:9-10). The word "lest" *(pen)* appears in the Eden story, along with the words *"hein"* and *"ve-atah,"* articulating God's concern that the human being might eat of the Tree of Life (Genesis 3:22). It appears also in the Babel story, together with the word "come" *(havah)*, in a complex interplay that bears spelling out before returning to the implications of the appearance of these words in our story.

The tower builders use the word *"havah"* twice, first introducing their plan to make brick and mortar (11:3) and then introducing their plan to build the city and the tower that would reach the heavens (11:4). The latter plan is articulated along with the concern that the building project is designed to address: "lest *(pen)* we be scattered on the face of all the earth." The word *"havah"* appears a third time to introduce God's response to the state of humanity (introduced by *"hein"*) and to the threat of a human race unencumbered by limitations on their future plans and achievements (introduced by *"ve-atah,"* 11:6-7). The implication of the triple use of this word is that, while the tower builders seek to be godlike, God asserts God's own absolute dominion by destroying their plan and making such plans impossible in the future. No matter how high they try to build, as Umberto Cassuto and others have pointed out, God notices them far *down* below from God's supernal abode and decides to come *down* in order to examine their doings and respond to them (11:5-7).

Pharaoh's use of the words "*hein*," "*ve-atah*," "*pen*," and "*havah*," at the very beginning of the enslavement narrative and in the story of the bricks, situates Pharaoh as a person who seeks to take the place of God. From the perspective of the story of the tower builders, Pharaoh is both like the human beings who seek to reach divine heights and like God, ensuring that his own dominion is absolute.

Pharaoh's aspiration and the parallel between his story and the story of the tower builders is captured by Isaiah in a prophecy that juxtaposes the story of the Tower of Babel with the story of the Egyptian enslavement. The prophecy includes a taunt that is directed against the king of Babylon, which is to be delivered "on the day when the Lord gives you rest from your sorrow and trouble and from the hard labor that you have been made to labor" (Isaiah 14:3). "The hard labor" (*ha-avodah ha-kashah*) recalls the Israelites' "hard labor" in Egypt (Exodus 1:14; 6:9) – as does reference to enforced labor or enslavement. The opening words of the taunt—"How the oppressor (*nogeis*) has ceased (*shavat*)!" (Isaiah 14:4)—echo elements of the story of the brickmaking for Pharaoh. Worrying that Moses and Aaron are causing the people to "cease (*ve-hishbatem*) from their burdensome labor," Pharaoh instructed the taskmasters (*nogsim* – literally, "oppressors") to carry out his intensified plan of oppression (Exodus 5:5-6). Isaiah, then, figures the Babylonian king as a Pharaoh who enslaves and oppresses the people but whose oppression, as Pharaoh had feared about the oppression that he himself had imposed, will one day come to cease.

The prophecy itself contrasts Babylon's ambition with its anticipated downfall. "But you said in your heart: 'I will ascend to the skies, above the stars of God I will raise my throne… I will ascend on the heights of a cloud, I will be like the Most High'" (Isaiah 14:13-14). Instead, the prophecy continues, Babylon will be brought down to the deepest depths (14:15). Describing this downfall in great detail, the prophecy draws to a conclusion by describing Babylon's extirpation in a pair of alliterative phrases: "'I will cut off from Babylon name and remnant (*shem u-sh'ar*), offshoot and offspring (*ve-nin va-nekhed*),' declares the Lord" (14:22).

Babylon's aspirations and collapse recall the story that gave Babylon its name. The tower builders' goal was to reach the heavens and to make themselves a name so that they not be scattered on the face of the earth (Genesis 11:4). God comes down and confuses their language, scattering them on the face of the earth, so that they stop building the city (11:7-8). The story concludes ironically by explaining that Babylon *did* receive a name through this incident, the name "Babel" evoking the confusion of language and the scattering that God had imposed on the tower builders (11:9).

In fact, the word "name" (*shem*) is central to this story, played on by the repeated use of the consonantally identical word "there" (*sham*). The latter word appears five times in the story (vv. 2, 7, 8, 9 [twice]), for a total of seven occurrences of *"shem"* and *"sham."* The tower builders want to situate themselves *there*, but God scatters them *from there*; the tower builders want to make for themselves a *name*, but God disrupts their plan by imposing the confusion that gives them the *name* Babylon.

The word *"shem"* is especially significant because the Tower of Babel story occurs right after the genealogy of Noah's three sons, ending with the family of Shem (Genesis 10), and right before the genealogy of Shem (11:10-26), which culminates with Abram, whose *name* (*shem*) God promises to make great (12:2). In contrast to this focus on Shem in the story's context, the tower-building story focuses on a different line of Noah's children, the family of Ham. The tower builders gather in the land of Shinar (11:2), a place associated with Nimrod, the descendant of Ham, as is the land of Babylon itself (10:10). Ham is also the progenitor of Mitzrayim—Egypt (10:6). Thus, among other things, the Tower of Babel story serves to contrast the overweening aspirations of the descendants of Ham with the destiny of the descendants of Shem.

It is this story that serves as the basis for Isaiah's prophecy against Babylon, a prophecy in which he describes the king of Babylon in words that recall the oppression inflicted on the Israelites by Pharaoh. Isaiah's juxtaposition of Babel's origin story with the story of the Egyptian enslavement highlights the parallel between the two stories and underscores the fact that Pharaoh's plan of oppressive enslavement casts Pharaoh as one who would be godlike and who seeks to quash the aspirations of his human subjects.

The stories of the brickmaking and the tower-building share several additional elements besides the word pattern common to these stories. First, and most obvious, the two stories are about manufacturing bricks; in fact, each uses a form of the verb-noun pair *lilbon leveinim*—literally, "to brick bricks" (Genesis 11:3; Exodus 5:7 – the verb, in fact, appears only in these two passages). The making of bricks in the Babel story is particularly interesting, because, while introduced with one of the occurrences of the word "*havah*," it does not have a stated goal. The people engage in a common enterprise to manufacture building blocks, producing human-made substitutes for natural building materials (Genesis 11:3). It is only after they manufacture these materials that they state their goal and their purpose, again using the word *havah*: they plan to build a city and tower reaching the heavens so as to make themselves a name so that they not be scattered (11:4). As the events are narrated, the people first go to work producing something with no particular goal in mind. It is the manufacture of these materials that seems to prompt a plan of what to do with them.

This skewed relationship between work and the goals toward which that work is directed is another element shared by our two stories. In the Babel story, rather than the goal necessitating the labor of producing the components that will allow the people to achieve that goal, the people start with the labor of production. Once they have produced the bricks—the stuff of which buildings can be made—the people think what they would like to build and what purpose that building might have. In Egypt, buildings will be built with the bricks, but the goal of the work is not those buildings. The purpose of the work is the act of labor itself, Pharaoh's desire to oppress his slaves and to crush them from aspiring to do anything other than serve him.

A third shared element is the motif of scattering. The tower builders fear that they will "be scattered (*nafutz*) over the face of the whole earth (*kol ha-aretz*)" (11:4 – compare 10:18, where the word "scatter" [*nafotzu*] is used in reference to the Canaanites, also descendants of Ham). In response, God indeed "scatters (*va-yafetz*) them over the face of the whole earth" so that they stop their building project (11:8). Pharaoh's demand that the Israelites go out and gather their own straw for the manufacture of bricks causes the people to scatter (*va-yafetz*) "throughout the whole land of (*be-khol eretz*) Egypt" (Exodus 5:12). The scattering is not incidental to Pharoah's plan. Pharaoh *decenters* the Israelites by imposing on them heavy labor, keeping them from joining together in common purpose to advance their own aspirations.

THE MANNA

"You are causing them to cease from their labors… let the labor be heavier (*tikhbad*)!" (Exodus 5:5, 9). Forms of the root *k-v-d* ("heavy" or "weighty") recur throughout the Exodus narrative, and the contest between Pharaoh and God can be traced through different uses and connotations of the word. A few examples will set the stage for the discussion of the other narratives about work to which we will turn soon.

Shortly after the story of the bricks and the episode in which God discloses the name Y-H-V-H to Moses and the Israelites (Exodus 6:2-6), Moses's mother's name is revealed to be Yokheved (6:20). The name Yokheved signifies God's *kavod*—glory (literally, "heaviness" or "weightiness"). At the Red Sea, God asserts that God will "be glorified (*ve-ikavdah*) by means of Pharaoh" and that "Egypt will know that I am the Lord in my glorification (*be-hikavdi*) by means of Pharaoh" (14:17-18; see also 14:4). And the book of Exodus ends with God's glory (*kavod*), which had earlier rested on Mount Sinai (24:16-17), filling the *mishkan* (tabernacle) that the Israelites constructed (40:34).

Pharaoh also famously becomes "heavy" – as God tells Moses, "The heart of Pharaoh is heavy (*kaveid*); he refuses to send the people" (7:14– see also 8:11, 28; 9:7, 34; 10:1). In response, when the Israelites finally leave and the Egyptians chase after them, God causes the Egyptian chariots to "drive heavily (*bi-khveidut*)" (14:25), eventually drowning the oppressors in the sea. The heaviness that Pharaoh sought to impose upon the Israelites, then, ultimately crushes the Egyptians. Meanwhile, Exodus is bookended with references to God's glory (*kavod*), a glory which is enhanced through the downfall of Pharaoh and the Egyptians.

But the first time that God's glory appears is not when the *mishkan* is erected, nor at the Sinaitic revelation. It first appears in the story of the manna.

Shortly after leaving Egypt, the Israelites travel from an oasis with springs and date trees and find themselves in the wilderness of Sin. Complaining against Moses, they recall the food that was available to them in Egypt, and worry that they have been condemned to death by starvation in the desert (15:27-16:3). God tells Moses of God's plan to rain down for the Israelites bread from the heavens, and Moses informs the people of this plan (16:4-5). But, before explaining that they will be fed by the hand of God, Moses tells the people: "In the evening you will know that the Lord took you out of Egypt, and in the morning you will see the glory of the Lord..." (16:6-7). No sooner do the people hear that God has responded to their complaints, than they turn toward the wilderness "and behold, the glory of the Lord appeared in the cloud" (16:9-10).

And so, if the crushing labor (*tikhbad ha-avodah*) of gathering straw to manufacture bricks left no room for awareness or service of God, the manna affords the very first opportunity for the Israelites to perceive God's glory (*kavod*). In fact, Pharaoh's concern that Moses and Aaron, by asking for the people to go and worship the Lord, are causing the Israelites to cease (*ve-hishbatem*) from their burdens is matched in the manna story by the centrality of Shabbat—a day on which "the people ceased (*va-yishbetu*)" (16:30) from their work of gathering and preparing their food.

The manna story, then, can be read as a counterpoint to the story of the brickmaking. It is the first extended narrative about the Israelites after they are delivered from their lives of enslavement, and it describes in great detail a different way of working and of relating to work.

In each of these stories, the Israelites need to go out and gather things. And, in each story, there is an amount of work that needs to be done each day—*devar yom be-yomo*, "each day's quantity on that day" (5:19; 16:4). Yet, no sooner than God tells Moses of the daily quota of manna that is to be gathered, God explains that on Friday the people will be preparing what they gather and so they will need to gather double that daily amount (16:5). Later, when double the daily amount of manna is indeed gathered on Friday, the people learn about Shabbat, the day on which there will be no manna to gather and on which they are not to work to prepare their food (16:22-26).

The instructions for gathering the daily quota of manna, then, include the idea that there will be cessation from labor. And the daily quota that needs to be gathered is based on need; each person is to gather the amount that they need to eat, an *omer* for each member of their household (16:16). This gathering is in stark contrast to the work of gathering the straw to manufacture the bricks. In that case, the daily quota of bricks was meant to be oppressive—to demand more and harder work than any of the slaves would be able to do. And the straw-gathering and brickmaking, as we saw, were not directed toward an intrinsic goal, nor of course did the work serve the purposes of the laborers themselves. Instead, the goal of the work was to enslave and oppress, to keep the people subjugated to Pharaoh. In contrast, the manna gathering is purposeful—to fulfill the essential human need of sustenance of the gatherers and their families.

Gathering the manna, then, offers a model of work that differs from the labor of the enslaved Israelites in relation to the elements of cessation from work, quantity and intensity, and purposefulness. In addition, while the labor that Pharaoh imposed caused the Israelites to scatter throughout the entire land of Egypt, the manna gathering centers the people around and inside the camp. The manna falls around the periphery of the camp (16:13-14); the people go out each morning to gather it and then bring it back home to prepare it and feed their families. And, on Shabbat, the people are not to go out at all; they are to stay in their place and enjoy the manna that they gathered and prepared the day before (16:22-30). The manna demarcates the camp, centering the Israelites within their community and their homes.

If Pharaoh's plan scattered the people and made sure that they not cease from their heavy work so that they "not pay attention to deceitful words" (5:9), the work of gathering and preparing the manna does the opposite. The breaks from work, centering in community, and opportunity to stay in place enable the people, focused now on their own basic survival, to structure their lives so as to make room for other things as well. While their energies are directed on securing necessities for themselves and their families, they now have a Shabbat—a time in which to be home and in community, and not to occupy themselves with work or with concern for their necessities.

The manna itself, of course, calls the Israelites' attention to God (16:6-10). It is a form of revelation and of assurance of God's presence with the people in the wilderness. The Israelites do not know what the thing is that appears in the wilderness surrounding the camp. Their lack of knowledge echoes Pharaoh's denial of knowledge of the Lord in the brickmaking story. But, unlike Pharaoh, who declares his lack of knowledge of Y-H-V-H, the Israelites ask a question: "What is it (*man hu*)?" The name of the substance, manna or *man*, expresses their curiosity, a recognition that there is something that they do not know, which opens a space for Moses to explain: "This is the bread that the Lord has given you to eat" (16:15). Indeed, God has already told Moses that God's gift of food will enable the Israelites to know "that I am the Lord your God" (16:12).

The story of the manna, then, is a first step in the Israelites' journey toward living in God's presence. In fact, the manna story foreshadows the narrative of the *mishkan*, the place that enables God's continued revelation to and presence among the people and the subject of the final story about work in the book of Exodus. A surprising number of expressions appear in both of these narratives, suggesting that the Israelites' experience with the manna is deeply connected with, and can be seen as paving the way for, the *mishkan* and the divine service that is centered there.

Moses tells the people that God will give them meat in the evening and bread in the morning (*ba-erev... ba-boker*, 16:8), and the people gather the manna each morning (*ba-boker ba-boker*, 16:21). These pairs of words appear later in relation to the divine service. The incense is to be burned each morning (*ba-boker ba-boker*) as well as each evening (*bein ha-arbayim*, 30:7-8), and the *tamid* sacrifice too is to be brought each morning and evening (29:39). And, when the work of constructing the *mishkan* is about to begin, the Israelites bring offerings "for the work of the service of the sanctuary" each morning (*ba-boker ba-boker*, 36:3).

Moses tells the people to gather the manna according to the number of persons in each household, an *omer* measure for each person. The people do as they are told, some gathering more and some less (*ha-marbeh ve-ha-mam'it*). When they measure what they have gathered, the one who had gathered more (*ha-marbeh*) had no more than he needed, and the one who had gathered less (*ha-mam'it*) had no less that he needed (16:16-18). Right after the instructions concerning the incense altar, God instructs Moses about the half shekel that each adult male is to give toward the service of the *mishkan*. The rich are not to give more (*lo yarbeh*), and the poor are not to give less (*lo yam'it*); each person is to donate precisely the same amount as an atonement gift toward the service of the *mishkan* (30:11-16).

The regularity of food gathering, then, and the notion that each person is allotted the same amount, regardless of capacity, is mirrored in the regularity of offerings to God and the uniformity of the atonement gift that each (adult male) Israelite is to give toward the service of the *mishkan*. And the specific quantity of manna, the *omer*, mirrors the gift of the first sheaf (*omer*) of grain that is harvested each spring, which the Israelites, once they come into the promised land, are to bring to the priest (Leviticus 23:9-11).

The prohibition against leaving over any of the manna until the morning (Exodus 16:19) recalls the rule against leaving over any of the Pesah sacrifice until morning (12:10). Other sacrifices, as well, are not to be left over until the morning following the time in which they are to be eaten; whatever is left over must be burned. This rule is articulated, among other places, in relation to the sacrifice brought at the inauguration of Aaron and his sons as priests (Exodus 29:34; Leviticus 8:32).

Another link between the manna and both the Pesah sacrifice and the inauguration of the priests is the word *mishmeret*, guarding. The double portion of manna gathered on Friday is to be eaten on that day as well as left over as a *mishmeret* for the following day, Shabbat (Exodus 16:23). In addition, Moses instructs the people to set aside an *omer* of manna as a *mishmeret* for future generations (16:32-34). The animal chosen for the Pesah sacrifice is to be set aside as a *mishmeret* until 14th Nisan (12:6). And Aaron and his sons are to remain at the entrance to the Tent of Meeting for seven days, keeping the Lord's *mishmeret* (Leviticus 8:35). The word also appears numerous times in the book of Numbers in relation to the *mishkan*, the work of the priests and the Levites, and the encampment of the entire community around the *mishkan* (e.g. Numbers 4:31-32; 31:30, 47).

Finally, the manna is described as resting on the ground like frost (*kefor*, Exodus 16:14). The rare word "*kefor*" in this sense appears elsewhere in the Bible only in poetic texts (Psalm 147:16; Job 38:29). But the letters of this rare word (*k-f-r*) recall the word "atone," which appears throughout biblical passages relating to the *mishkan* and to sacrifices, as well as to the half shekel atonement gift (Exodus 30:11-16), which, as we've seen, echoes the manna story. The root appears as well in the word "*kaporet*," the covering of the ark and seat of the cherubs in the inner sanctum of the *mishkan* (25:17-22; 26:34), as well as in relation to the yearly atonement ritual at the incense altar (30:10).

This panoply of words and phrases that the manna story shares with the work of constructing the *mishkan* and with instructions for divine service underscores the notion that the manna episode is a stage in the Israelites' development as a people who strive to live in God's presence and to serve God—to experience and respond to God's *kavod*. Echoing as it does both the straw-gathering story and the *mishkan* narrative, the manna story also stands as an intermediate step in the different experiences of work that are described in the book of Exodus.

THE MISHKAN

The final story about work in the book of Exodus tells of the building of the *mishkan*, a project that stands in sharp contrast with the enslaved Israelites' work building for Pharaoh at the beginning of the book.

The instructions for the *mishkan* begin with a call for materials. God lists for Moses the metals, fibers, skins, wood, oil, and precious stones that will be needed to make the sanctuary in which God will dwell amidst the people (Exodus 25:3-8). Moses is to take these materials as offerings "from each person whose heart makes them willing" (25:2). When the time comes to begin the project, Moses repeats God's instructions, calling upon "each person willing of heart" to bring offerings, and inviting "each person who is wise of heart" to come and fabricate the elements of the *mishkan* from these materials (35:5, 10). In response, each person "whose heart stirred them and whose spirit was willing" brought offerings (35:21). More specifically, men and women brought their jewelry, men who had yarn or skins brought them, the chieftains brought precious stones and spices, and women "who were wise of heart" spun precious yarns and brought them (35:22-29).

Moses then informs the people that God has called an individual by name: Bezalel son of Uri son of Hur will lead the construction effort, assisted by Oholiab son of Ahisamach. These two men have special abilities of craftsmanship as well as in teaching, and they are charged with leading "each person who is wise of heart, in whose heart the Lord gave wisdom, each person whose heart stirred them" in doing the work (35:30-36:2).

The *mishkan*, then, is built through the efforts of many people but, notably, different people do different things. Each person brings the resources that he or she has, each person contributes the skills that he or she has, and each person offers materials and labor according to how each person's heart moves them.

In this regard, the work of building the *mishkan* differs from both the brickmaking story and the story of the manna. In both of those stories, there is no distinction between individuals. In the brickmaking story, individuals are blurred into a mass of people who need to meet a quota of work that is imposed on them. In the story of the manna, each person is distinct and works toward the quota of food that is needed for their own family, but there is no sense of individuality; everyone is called upon to do exactly the same kind of work. The *mishkan* is the first time that we are offered a vision of people as individuals with different abilities and inclinations, and that we see people individually motivated to step forward and contribute, each in their own way, toward the work that is to be done. The foundation of the *mishkan*, in fact, is constructed out of the half shekel that each Israelite male identically donated—the silver was mostly used to cast the sockets of the boards and posts of the sanctuary (38:25-28). But the remainder of the *mishkan* and its furnishings reflect the individual gifts, talents, and inclinations of the people.

The appointment of Bezalel and Oholiab highlights this new focus on individuality. Out of the haze of sameness that characterizes the brickmaking and manna stories, individuals now emerge, called by name and described in relation to their distinctive abilities. This naming of the leaders of the work effort is particularly striking in a book that begins with the names of the children of Israel (1:1-3), but in which their descendants are enslaved by a Pharaoh who sees them simply as a too-numerous mass of people (1:9; 5:5). Finally now, in relation to the work that is to be done in constructing the *mishkan*, individuals are called forth by name.

The focus on names recalls the Tower of Babel story as well. There, as we saw, the people sought to make for themselves a name (*shem*), and the story plays on the idea of a name with the naming of Babylon and the sandwiching of the story between two genealogies of Shem, the second culminating with the introduction of Abram, the descendant of Shem whose name (*shem*) God will make great. In the Babel story, which foreshadows the story of the brickmaking, everyone is the same—the people want to make a name for themselves as a group, but there are no individuals in the story; everyone is "of one language and of one speech" (Genesis 11:1). The interruption of the people's plan and the scattering of the people over the face of the earth makes way for the foregrounding of the narrative of the descendants of Shem, their enslavement in Egypt, and their redemption by the God whom they are destined to serve. And now, as they embark on a project to build a sanctuary for God, they emerge not just as a nation in God's service but as a group of individuals, each of whom brings their distinctive self to the work.

Another point of comparison between the *mishkan* story and the stories of the brickmaking and the manna is the physical orientation of the people and the direction of their movement. The brickmaking causes the people to scatter throughout the land of Egypt, much as the Babel story ends in the scattering of the tower builders. In contrast, we noted, the manna demarcates the camp; the people go out to gather the manna and then return to the camp with the food that will sustain their families. And on Shabbat, when the manna does not fall, the people stay in their place. Nevertheless, there is no center to the community—neither a physical center nor something toward which it is oriented.

The *mishkan*, for the first time, provides such a center. "They will make for me a sanctuary, and I will dwell in their midst," God explains, as God instructs Moses to ask the people to bring the materials that will be needed for this project (Exodus 25:8). The *mishkan* is quite literally in the center of the camp, as is described in detail in Numbers 2. It is the center, in addition, in that all the Israelites direct their efforts toward the work that is needed to fabricate the components of the *mishkan* and its furnishings.

In this sense, it is similar to the beginning of the Babel story, before the people are scattered when God interrupts their plan. But this similarity highlights the core difference between the two projects: the tower is designed for the glory of its builders, while the *mishkan* is built for God's glory. The tower builders want to reach the heavens; the *mishkan*'s goal is to enable God to dwell among the people on earth.

The *mishkan*, then, not only centers the people on a shared goal and physical locus; it centers the people's efforts on, and orients the community toward, something that is outside themselves. In this way, too, it is different from the manna story, in which the work that the people do is for themselves, to provide for their own and their families' basic needs. And so there is a trajectory from the brickmaking story to the manna story to the story of constructing the *mishkan*, in relation to the community having a center and an orientation toward something beyond themselves and their physical sustenance. While the labor of brickmaking left no room for awareness of God or divine service, and the manna offered the Israelites the first glimpse of God's glory, the *mishkan*, in which evidence of God's glory was visible to the Israelites throughout their travels in the wilderness, was also the locus of the Israelites' service of God.

Perhaps the most crucial difference between building God's sanctuary at the end of Exodus and doing the labor of manufacturing and construction for Pharaoh at the beginning of the book is the relationship between work and purpose. Pharaoh, we saw, hatches his plan of construction *in order* to enslave the Israelites. The work is designed to oppress the workers;

what is built is a by-product of Pharaoh's goal of enslavement. The work of the *mishkan*, in contrast, is directed toward a goal having to do with the product of the labor itself. When God tells Moses to ask the people to bring the precious materials, even before explaining the precise uses to which the materials will be put, God explains the purpose: to make a sanctuary for God so that God may dwell among the people. Articulation of its purpose precedes the work and motivates it.

Because the work is directed toward an intrinsic goal, there is a limit to how much work needs to be done. When the Israelites finally embark on the project and begin to bring the raw materials and to spin the fibers that will be needed for fabrication and construction of the *mishkan* and its furnishings (Exodus 35:21-29), it turns out that they continue to bring more than is needed. The artisans come to Moses and tell him: "the people are bringing more (*marbim*) than suffices for the labor of the work that the Lord has commanded to do." And Moses announces that the people should stop their work of preparing and bringing the materials (36:3-7).

The word "*marbim*"—to do or bring much or many—is noteworthy. The book of Exodus began with the notice that the children of Israel became many (*va-yirbu*, 1:7) and with Pharaoh's alarm at the numerousness (*rav*) of the people (1:9). Pharaoh implements his plan to enslave the Israelites "lest they become many (*pen yirbeh*)" (1:10) and, when Pharaoh later rejects Moses and Aaron's request to send the people to worship the Lord, he introduces his plan to intensify the Israelites' labor with the words "Behold, the people of the land now are many (*rabim*)" (5:5). The Israelites' numerousness is a problem for Pharaoh.

In the *mishkan* narrative, the word appears in the causative form: the Israelites are now subjects who act toward a goal; their *manyness* has been transmuted to the choice to do *much* work toward a shared purpose. It is that purpose which either necessitates action or renders action unnecessary. When the work is sufficient for the purpose that motivates it and toward which it is directed, there is no need to labor further: "the work was sufficient to do all of the work, and more so" (36:7).

The *mishkan*'s very structure highlights its purposefulness as well. Unlike the Tower of Babel or Pharaoh's cities, the *mishkan* is not built of brick; it is assembled out of boards and curtains. It is a tent, not a building. It is not meant to stand permanently; it is meant to be put together or taken apart as the people follow the cloud of glory that indicates when they should encamp and when they should break camp and travel through the

Work and Its Purposes

wilderness. Sometimes, that is, the *mishkan* as a built structure is simply not there; it is re-assembled each time the Israelites pause their travels and set up camp, in order to make a place where God can dwell in the midst of the community.

In fact, Ramban (Naḥmanides) notes that the instructions for fabricating the *mishkan* begin with the furnishings, in particular the ark and its covering (*kaporet*), from above which God will continue to reveal God's word to the people (25:10-22). Bezalel, on the other hand, begins the work with the curtains and the boards that will form the tent inside which the ark and the other furnishings will be placed (36:8-38). While practically it makes sense to build the structure first, before fabricating the furnishings that will be placed inside it, Ramban points out, God's instructions make clear that the structure is not the key element of the *mishkan*. It is simply a framework within which the *mishkan*'s purpose can be realized (Ramban, Introduction to Exodus 25).

SHABBAT

The final point of comparison between the Israelites' work for Pharaoh, the gathering of the manna, and the work of building the *mishkan* is the notion of Shabbat or cessation of labor. As we saw, Pharaoh wants to make sure that the Israelites have no cessation from labor; he worries that Moses and Aaron are causing this now-numerous people to cease (*ve-hishbatem*) from their burdens. In the manna story, on the other hand, Shabbat is central: the people gather a double portion of manna on Friday and are to prepare their food in advance for Shabbat, a day on which they will neither go out to gather food nor work to prepare it.

The instructions for the *mishkan* and the work of building the *mishkan* are framed by passages about Shabbat. At the end of the instructions and the notice that God has appointed Bezalel and inspired him with the understanding that will enable him to lead the work, God conveys to Moses an extended teaching about Shabbat that Moses is to transmit to the people (Exodus 31:12-17). And, after the narrative interlude about the sin of the Golden Calf and its aftermath, when Moses finally is about to instruct the people about the work of the *mishkan*, Moses begins by gathering the people and telling them about the prohibition of work on Shabbat (35:1-3).

Furthermore, as many ancient and modern readers have noted, the description of the work of the *mishkan* echoes the story of creation. In particular, the notice that the work of the *mishkan* was completed (*va-teikhel*, 39:32) echoes the completion of creation (*va-yekhulu*, Genesis 2:1), and Moses's seeing and evaluating all of the work that the Israelites had accomplished (Exodus 39:43) echoes God's seeing and evaluating all that which God had made (Genesis 1:31). The implication is that the work of constructing the *mishkan* parallels the work of world-creation. If so, then it is not only that *cessation from work* on Shabbat corresponds to God's *cessation from the work* of creation on Shabbat, as implied in the passage about Shabbat with which the instructions to build the *mishkan* culminates: "because for six days the Lord made the heavens and the earth, and on the seventh day he ceased and was refreshed" (Exodus 31:17). It is that cessation from the work of *building the mishkan* corresponds to God's cessation from the work of *creation of the world*. And, if God commands us to cease working on Shabbat as God ceased the work of creation on Shabbat, then the *kind of work* that we do throughout the six days of labor (*sheshet yemei ha-ma'aseh*) and from which we must cease on Shabbat, is work that is like the work of building the *mishkan*.

This is the insight that shapes the Talmud's approach to delineating the kind of work that is forbidden on Shabbat. The Mishnah (Shabbat 7:2) lists the forbidden labors, thirty-nine acts that constitute, and are grouped by, activities done in the service of basic needs, such as food, clothing, and shelter. Labor performed to meet basic needs is the kind of labor that was done in the story of the manna, the first episode in which the newly-freed Israelites are instructed about cessation of labor on Shabbat. In fact, while Mishnah Shabbat delineates thirty-nine labors, the greater part of the tractate addresses specifically those labors that are involved in food preparation and in moving objects from one domain to another, while Mishnah Shabbat's partner tractate, Eruvin, focuses both on moving objects from place to place and on *teḥum shabbat*, the restriction on traveling more than a set distance beyond one's place of residence on Shabbat. These are the very acts that the Israelites needed to do in order to gather the manna and prepare it for eating, and the very acts that they are instructed to desist from on Shabbat and to perform in preparation for Shabbat (Exodus 16:23, 26, 29).

The Talmud, on the other hand, links the prohibited labors to the *mishkan*:

> That which is taught in the Mishnah:
> "The categories of work are forty less one"—
> to what does this correspond?
> Rabbi Ḥanina bar Ḥama said to them:
> "Corresponding to the labor-acts of the *mishkan*." ...
>
> It is taught in a *baraita* in accordance with the one who said,
> "Corresponding to the labor-acts of the *mishkan*,"
> as it is taught:
> One is liable only for work that there was one like it in the *mishkan*:
>
>> They sowed, and you may not sow.
>> They reaped, and you may not reap.
>> They lifted the boards from the ground to the wagon,
>> and you may not bring things in
>> from the public domain to the private domain.
>> They lowered the boards from the wagon to the ground,
>> and you may not bring things out
>> from the private domain into the public domain.
>
> *Bavli Shabbat 49b*

The *baraita* focuses specifically on work that is done for the purposes of food production and on the act of moving objects between the public and private domains, the spheres of labor that are forbidden in the manna story and on which tractates Shabbat and Eruvin focus. But the *baraita* links these forbidden labors not to the manna story, but to the *mishkan*, corroborating Rabbi Ḥanina bar Ḥama's teaching that the thirty-nine forbidden categories of labor correspond to the work of the *mishkan*.

The talmudic linking of the labors forbidden on Shabbat to the *mishkan* is continuous with the juxtaposition of *mishkan* and Shabbat in the book of Exodus and with the echoing of the creation narrative in the description of the work of the *mishkan* and its completion. Classical commentators note the word *akh* ("but" or "only"), which introduces the teaching about Shabbat that concludes God's instructions about the *mishkan* and its furnishings (Exodus 31:13). This disjunctive suggests, according to Ramban for example: "Do the work of the Tent of Meeting but guard my Sabbaths forever; and in Torat Kohanim (the Sifra) it says: you might think that the building of the Temple pushes Shabbat aside, but the Torah teaches 'Guard my Sabbaths and fear my sanctuary; I am the Lord' (Leviticus 19:30; 26:2)." Ramban understands the parallel between Shabbat and the sanctuary, suggested in a verse that appears twice in Leviticus, like the disjunctive juxtaposition of Shabbat and *mishkan* in Exodus, as implying a prohibition: creation of the *mishkan* is not to push Shabbat aside. From this it is a small step to infer that, when thinking about what kind of work is forbidden on Shabbat *in general*, we might look at what kind of work is forbidden in the *mishkan* and extrapolate from that the categories of labor from which one must desist on Shabbat.

But the Talmud's generation of the laws of forbidden labor on Shabbat from the *mishkan* goes beyond the suggestion that the thirty-nine forbidden labors are the acts that were essential to the work of constructing the *mishkan*. The Talmud looks to the work of the *miskhan* as delineating, in addition, the *nature* of work acts that are forbidden on Shabbat. The Talmud introduces the concept of *melekhet mahshevet* as the criterion that determines whether the act that one has done, even if it falls under one of the thirty-nine categories of labor, is the kind of work that is biblically forbidden on Shabbat. *Melekhet mahshevet asrah torah*, the Talmud asserts in a number of places: only work that has the specific attributes of *melekhet mahshevet* is forbidden by the Torah to be performed on Shabbat (Bavli Beitzah 13b, Hagigah 10b, Bava Kama 26b, 60a).

The term *melekhet mahshevet* derives from the story of the *mishkan*'s construction. After the people have brought their various offerings, God tells Moses that God has called Bezalel to lead the work of craftsmanship and construction:

> [31]And he has filled him with the spirit of God,
> in wisdom, in understanding, and in knowledge,
> and in all manner of work.
> [32]*Ve-lahshov mahshavot*,
> to work in gold, and in silver, and in copper.
> [33]And in the cutting of stones, to set them,
> and in carving of wood,
> to make all manner of *melekhet mahshevet*.
> [34]And he has put in his heart that he may instruct,

he and Oholiab the son of Ahisamach of the tribe of Dan.
³⁵He has filled them with wisdom of heart,
to do all manner of work of the engraver,
and of the *ḥoshev*, and of the embroiderer, in blue and in purple,
in scarlet and in fine linen, and of the weaver,
of those that do any work, and of *ḥoshvei maḥshavot*.

Exodus 35:31-35 (see also 31:1-5)

The root *ḥ-sh-v* appears over and over again in this short passage, in both verb and noun forms: Bezalel has the capacity *laḥshov maḥshavot*, and the various kinds of craftsmanship are described as the work of *ḥoshvei maḥshavot*. And all of the kinds of work that are to be done to craft the *mishkan*'s components and furnishings are described as *melekhet maḥshevet*.

The term *melekhet maḥshevet* is variously rendered in Bible translations as inventive work, artistic workmanship, skillful workmanship, and artistic craft, among other phrases. The word pair seems to connote the element of *design*—design both in the sense of a purposeful plan and in the sense of work that conforms to that plan. Bezalel and the craftspeople that he instructs have the ability to imagine the work that needs to be done, and the ability to shape their work in accordance with their purposes and intentions.

Bezalel is able to lead this work because he is inspired with "the spirit of God"—*ruaḥ elohim*. This term once again evokes the story of creation: at the very beginning of Genesis, as God is about to perform the first act of creation, we are told that *ruaḥ elohim* was hovering over the chaotic waters (Genesis 1:2). Now that same divine spirit inspires the human being who is responsible for designing and crafting the *mishkan*.

Fascinatingly, the word *maḥshavot*, the thoughts or designs that Bezalel and his craftspeople are able to imagine and to bring to fruition, appears only one other time in the Torah – at the moment that God becomes disappointed in the human beings that God has created, and as the world is about to be plunged into the chaos of the Flood. "The Lord saw that the evil of the human being was great on the earth and that every plan of the thoughts (*maḥshavot*) of his heart was only evil all the time" (6:5). While, in the creation story, God saw over and over again that the world that was being created was good, now God sees the evil of human beings, and that evil is characterized as the plans or designs of the human beings' *mahshavot*. That Bezalel and his craftspeople are *hoshvei mahshavot*, that human beings now plan the creative work of constructing the place in which God will dwell, brings us full circle. Instead of the world-destroying designs of the human beings in Genesis, the designs of Bezalel and his workers generate a new creation. The building of the *mishkan* is a world-building act, a project that parallels the creation of the world, this time by a human being infused with *ruah elohim*.

The talmudic category of *melekhet mahshevet* builds on the notions of purpose, craftsmanship, and creativeness implicit in the Torah's description of the work of the *mishkan*. The category is understood by the Talmud and its commentators to exclude a variety of acts that, although they fall under the categories of labor that are forbidden, fail to exhibit the qualities of the work that was performed in the construction of the *mishkan*. Such acts may lack intentionality or purposefulness, or they may be destructive rather than constructive, or they may be inconsequential (impermanent or incomplete), or they may be done in a manner that is indirect or that is not consonant with the work of a craftsperson.

Perhaps the primary example of work that falls outside of the category of *melekhet mahshevet* is *melakhah she-einah tzerikhah le-gufah*—"work that is not needed for itself" (Hagigah 10a-b). Talmudic commentators differ as to the precise understanding of this category of acts, but the category suggests that, even if one intentionally performs a labor that is prohibited on Shabbat, the act violates Shabbat only if it fulfills the purpose of the person who performs it. That is, on Shabbat it is not only intentionality that is essential for culpability; the core attribute of forbidden work on Shabbat, rather, is purposefulness. If a labor is done for something other than the purpose that the person desires, or if it is done for a purpose that is ancillary to the quintessential purpose of that labor (see Tosafot on Hagigah 10b, s.v. *melekhet mahshevet*), it does not fulfill the definition of *melekhet mahshevet*, the kind of work that was performed in the construction of the *mishkan* and which is prohibited on Shabbat.

Purposeless work, though, is precisely the kind of work that Pharaoh had imposed on the Israelites. The making of bricks and the building of Pharaoh's cities, as we saw, were forced on the Israelites with the goal of enslaving and crushing them. The resulting Egyptian cities were not the *purpose* of the labor; they were merely the by-products of that labor. Purposefulness, the attribute that permeates the entire narrative of the instructions for building the *mishkan* and the work of fabrication and construction, is the very thing that is absent from the work of building with which the book of Exodus begins.

The book of Exodus, then, begins with *melakhah she-einah tzerikhah le-gufah* and concludes with *melekhet mahshevet*. At the end of the book, the Israelites, led by Bezalel, are able to envision what they are being asked to create and to bring that vision into reality. The work that they do is characterized by deep intentionality and by individual motivation to contribute toward a shared purpose.

PRACTICES AND STORIES

The Talmud's crafting of the laws of Shabbat in relation to the *mishkan* embeds the Exodus story within our practice and experience of Shabbat. As the culmination of the Exodus narrative, the building of the *mishkan* completes the trajectory of stories about work that begins with the Israelites' enslavement and continues through the story of the manna. The linking of Shabbat's forbidden labors with the labors involved in construction of the *mishkan*, and the characterization of forbidden work acts as those that meet the criteria of *melekhet mahshevet*, help us consider what kind of work is worthy of our efforts. What kind of work is world-building? What kind of work sustains individuals and community? What kind of work makes good use of our individual talents, resources, and inclinations? And what kind of work helps orient ourselves and our community toward something beyond our own needs?

Shabbat also helps us remember that work cannot be its own end. Both the manna story and the story of the *mishkan* set limits to work: the people are to gather just the amount of manna that they need, and Moses commands the people to cease bringing contributions to the *mishkan* once enough materials have been gathered. In each case, as we have seen, the work has a clearly articulated purpose, and so the work need not—and ought not—be continued when that purpose has been accomplished.

The focus on Shabbat in both of these passages communicates as well that work cannot be unceasing. In fact, the Talmud understands Moses's call to stop bringing materials to the *mishkan* as occurring in preparation for Shabbat (Bavli Shabbat 96b). Cessation from work enables us to consider the nature and purpose of work, to step back and imagine the world that we want to inhabit, so that the work that we do the rest of the week can be put to the purpose of building that world. Unlike the tower builders, who first did the work of manufacturing bricks and then were driven to do something with the bricks, and unlike the Israelites in Egypt, who were forced to work unceasingly so that they could never imagine a different way of being, we are given the opportunity and the charge to rest from work, to consider the kind of work from which we are resting on Shabbat, and to imagine to what purposes we want to dedicate our work during the rest of the week.

> [12]Keep the Sabbath day to sanctify it,
> as the Lord your God has commanded you.
> [13]Six days you shall labor and do all your work.
> [14]But the seventh day is the Sabbath of the Lord your God;
> you shall not do any work, you or your son or your daughter,
> or your male or female slave,
> or your ox or your ass or any of your cattle,
> or the stranger that is within your gates,
> in order that your male and female slave may rest as you do.
> [15]And remember that you were a slave in the land of Egypt
> and the Lord your God took you out from there
> with a mighty hand and an outstretched arm;
> therefore the Lord your God has commanded you
> to observe the Sabbath day.
>
> *Deuteronomy 5:12-15*

In Moses's retelling of the Ten Commandments in the book of Deuteronomy, the practice of Shabbat is meant to remind us of a story, and it is also a call to action. Shabbat, here, is a protest against tyranny and oppression, against the kind of labor that diminishes those who do it. We are to make sure that others in our midst are not subject to the kind of oppressive labor to which Pharaoh subjected us. And we are to make sure, as well, that our own work is not oppressive—not just in the sense of hard work, but in the sense of work that is imposed on us, work that lacks purpose, work that is unceasing and that leaves no room for contemplation about what lies beyond the work that we do.

This is not just propositional knowledge; it is is experiential, imaginative knowing: "*Remember* that you were a slave." The practice of Shabbat calls to mind a set of stories, the interplay between them, and the ways in which they are refracted through the lens of rabbinic texts. Shabbat observances—from the two loaves on our table, recalling the double portion of manna in preparation for Shabbat, to the injunction not to travel beyond the Shabbat boundary, to the categories of forbidden labor and the criterion of *melekhet maḥshevet*—call us into the story of gathering the manna and the story of constructing the *mishkan*. Entering into these stories, we are invited to imagine not only the work from which we were freed—the work of our enslavement—but also the kinds of work in which we engaged during our journey from enslavement to freedom and the kinds of work to which we might choose to dedicate ourselves today.

TO KNOW AND BE KNOWN

> A new king arose over Egypt who did not know Joseph.
>
> *Exodus 1:8*

THE STORY OF the second book of the Torah begins with *not knowing*. After the introduction of the book of Exodus, which lists the names of the children of Israel, notes the death of Joseph and his brothers, and announces the exponential growth of the people, the notice about the king who *did not know* sets in motion the story that is to unfold. That the story of Israel's enslavement and becoming a nation—the story of the book of Exodus—begins with *not knowing* is especially striking because the first book of the Torah begins with the human being's coming into a condition of *knowing*, when Adam and Eve eat of the fruit of the Tree of Knowledge. That Pharaoh does *not* know, then, is problematic, and it is the problem of *not knowing* that sets the stage for what is to follow.

In fact, the theme of knowing or not knowing pervades the book of Exodus. People are said to know or not know other people; God is described as knowing people; and people either do or do not know God. Exodus has roughly the same number of references to knowledge as Genesis, the story of humanity's grappling with knowledge and with proper ways to know. Exodus' story of enslavement, redemption, and becoming God's people can be read as an unfolding of ways of knowing in a post-Edenic world. But before portraying what it means to have knowledge and what the purposes of knowledge might be, the book focuses in its early chapters on those who choose to know, those who choose not to know, and those who do not yet know.

CHOOSING TO KNOW

The introduction of the king who *does not know* motivates the plot of our story. Whether the verse means that the king did not know Joseph personally, or that the king chose not to recognize his debt to Joseph, or simply that the memory of Joseph and the help that he extended to Pharaoh had been forgotten, one thing is clear: the king's not knowing corresponds with the decision to harm Joseph's people. Not knowing is a moral stance; it means that the king will not act in gratitude toward Joseph's family—in fact, will not act even with the duty of care that a king has toward his subjects. Not knowing means that he will feel free to harm Joseph's family. From a place of not knowing, the king will unfold a plan of abuse, enslavement, and murder.

"I do not know" was uttered for the first time in the Torah by Cain. "Where is Abel your brother?" God asks, and Cain replies: "I *do not know*. Am I my brother's keeper?" (Genesis 4:9). The two parts of Cain's reply constitute a single claim. "I do not know" means I don't *have to* know—I'm not responsible for my brother. Not knowing, or claiming not to know, or choosing not to know, is a denial of moral responsibility.

Cain's denial of knowledge is especially notable in the context of the story that precedes it. Cain's father, Adam, is put in a garden that has in its center the Tree of Knowledge of Good and Evil. That tree, of all the trees in the garden, is off limits to Adam. But, of course, Eve and Adam eat the fruit of that tree, instantly becoming people who know (3:6-7). Once humanity is propelled into a state of knowing, knowing becomes a moral imperative. It is through knowing that a person can choose between good and evil, between the paths of blessing and of curse. A few chapters later, after the Flood, Noah will awaken into a state of knowledge and extend blessing and curse in relation to good and evil acts (9:24-27). So for Cain to deny knowledge—immediately after the Garden of Eden story—is deeply problematic. It is Cain's responsibility to know and to shape his behavior in line with the knowledge that he is now capable of possessing.

The story of the beginnings of humanity, then, begins with a movement between not knowing and knowing, and with a shift from knowledge being off limits to human beings to knowledge being available, and to knowing being a fundamental moral stance. It is all the more striking that Exodus, the story of the beginnings of the Israelites, begins with *not* knowing. Pharaoh's not knowing, like Cain's, is a denial of moral responsibility.

In contrast with Pharaoh's not knowing, in the next chapter Moses's sister chooses to know. When baby Moses is put in the river, "his sister took a stand far off *to know* what would be done to him" (Exodus 2:4). Moses's sister, of course, does not stand there merely to gather information about her brother's fate. She positions herself in a place of knowing so that she can help shape that fate.

It is noteworthy that she stations herself "far off" (*mei-rahok*), which is necessary in order for her not to be noticed, but that nevertheless she is positioning herself "to know." In Genesis, when Hagar sits at a distance (*harheik*), it is with the intention *not* to see what will happen to her child (Genesis 21:16). That Abraham, in the next chapter, is able to see from afar (*mei-rahok*) the place to which he and Isaac must go (22:4) is a testament to Abraham's vision—*even though* he is far away, he is able to see the place that God has chosen. So Moses's sister's ability to know despite being far off highlights her determination to know and to care. She takes responsibility for her brother, making sure, when Pharaoh's daughter finds him, that the baby will be returned to his mother. And returning the baby to his family will mean enabling him to become the redeemer of Israel: this child will grow up to recognize the Israelites as his brethren, to see their suffering, and, like his sister before him, to extend himself in care toward his brothers (Exodus 2:11-12).

Moses's sister, then, is the antithesis of Cain. While Cain chooses a stance of not knowing, of not being his brother's keeper, Moses's sister makes sure to know and to act to save her brother. She is also the antithesis of Pharaoh; his not knowing propels the story of enslavement, while her knowing sets the stage for redemption.

The sister's knowing also anticipates another knowing. The second chapter ends as the enslaved Israelites cry out and as their cry rises up to God. God hears the Israelites' groaning and remembers the covenant with the patriarchs. "And God saw the Children of Israel, and God *knew*" (2:23-25).

God's knowing is the culmination of God's hearing and seeing and remembering the covenant. This is an empathic knowledge, as God articulates to Moses right after, at the burning bush: "I have surely seen the affliction of my people who are in Egypt, and I have heard their cry on account of their taskmasters—for I know their sufferings" (3:7). God *senses* the people's suffering; God feels their pain. This relational, experiential knowledge leads God to take responsibility for them—"And I have come down to save them from the hand of Egypt" (3:8).

In the first three chapters of the book, then, Exodus sets out exemplars of not knowing and of knowing: Pharaoh, who does not know and hence enslaves and abuses the people; Moses's sister, who chooses to know and to assume a position of responsibility for her brother; and God, who knows the suffering of the people and is moved to save them. In each of these cases, what is known or not known is other people. But, as the narrative progresses, there will be an additional object of knowing or of not knowing – people will know or not know God.

KNOWLEDGE OF GOD

After the revelation at the burning bush (3:1-4:17), Moses and Aaron appear before Pharaoh for the first time, proclaiming the word of the Lord: "Let my people go" (5:1). Pharaoh replies: "Who is Y-H-V-H that I should listen to his voice to let Israel go? I *do not know* Y-H-V-H, and I will not let Israel go" (5:2). Like the Egyptian king with whom the book begins, who did not know Joseph, this Pharaoh denies knowledge of the Lord. Pharaoh's not knowing means that the king will not follow God's command concerning God's people. Once again, not knowing means not heeding the moral call.

Shortly after, God speaks to Moses and identifies Godself as Y-H-V-H. "I appeared to Abraham and to Isaac and to Jacob," God continues, "as E-l Shaddai, but by my name Y-H-V-H *did not make myself known* to them—*u-shmi y-h-v-h lo noda'ti lahem*" (6:2-3). The construction of the end of this verse is difficult. We might have expected "*u-vi-shmi y-h-v-h lo noda'ti lahem*" ("as" or "by means of" my name Y-H-V-H), parallel to be-*e-l shaddai* ("as" or "by means of" E-l Shaddai) earlier in the verse. God would then be saying that God appeared to the patriarchs as, or in the guise, of E-l Shaddai but did not make Godself known to them as Y-H-V-H. Alternatively, we might have expected *u-shmi y-h-v-h lo hoda'ti lahem*—I did not make known to them my name Y-H-V-H. Instead, the verse seems to be a hybrid of these two constructions; a literal translation would yield "but my name Y-H-V-H I did not make myself known to them." I will return to this difficult construction later. But, for now, it is noteworthy that here God, in a particular manifestation, has not yet become known to God's people, and it is God who has chosen not to make Godself known in that way.

God goes on to talk of the covenant that God established with the patriarchs and, in language that recalls the passage that led up to the revelation at the burning bush, to assert that, having heard the Israelites' moaning, God has remembered God's covenant (6:4-5). "Therefore say to the Children of Israel: I am Y-H-V-H" (6:6). Moses is asked to tell the Israelites God's name, the name in which God has not manifested to the patriarchs but now promises to manifest to the people. God pledges to take the people out of enslavement, to save them, to redeem them, and to take them as God's own people—actions described in what are traditionally referred to as the four expressions of redemption—"and you *will know* that I am Y-H-V-H your God who took you out…" (6:6-7).

This passage, then, speaks to a not knowing and to a promise of knowledge. God makes God's identity as Y-H-V-H known to the Israelites, and they will know that it is Y-H-V-H, their God, who redeemed them. Until now, by implication, they have not known Y-H-V-H. In fact, at the burning bush, Moses made this quite clear: "Behold, I will come to the Children of Israel, and I will say to them: 'The God of your fathers sent me to you.' And they will say to me: 'What is his name?'" Moses himself does not know how he might respond: "What will I say to them?" (3:13). It is then that God obliquely responds to Moses "*ehyeh asher ehyeh*… thus shall you say to the Children of Israel: '*ehyeh* sent me to you'" (3:14). And finally God says: "Thus shall you say to the Children of Israel: 'Y-H-V-H, the God of your fathers, the God of Abraham, the God of Isaac, and the God of Jacob sent me to you; this is my name for ever, and this is my appellation for all generations'" (3:15).

It turns out, then, that it is not only Pharaoh who does not know the Lord; the Israelites are ignorant of the Lord's identity as well. Moses worries that, if he tells the people that the God of their ancestors sent him, they will ask who that is. God reveals a particular name in response, but the question implies that the Israelites do not know God at all. Certainly, they do not know God as Y-H-V-H and, as God makes clear to Moses in chapter 6, God had in fact not yet manifested Godself, even to the patriarchs, as Y-H-V-H. But now, at the burning bush, God tells Moses this divine name and links the name with a mysterious statement about God's being—"*ehyeh asher ehyeh*," a first-person rendering of the name Y-H-V-H. And, spelling out to Moses in chapter 6 how God will fulfill the covenant established with the patriarchs, God once again identifies as Y-H-V-H, asserting that, at the culmination of the deliverance from Egyptian enslavement, the people will know that it is Y-H-V-H who redeemed them.

God's announcement of the divine name in these early chapters of Exodus, then, is anticipatory. It is not yet possible for the people to understand God as Y-H-V-H; God informs them of the divine name, but at this point God is merely giving them information, not understanding. God's manifestation as Y-H-V-H will unfold over the course of the book, as God fulfills the covenantal promise of deliverance. And, as we shall see, it will continue to unfold as God becomes present among the people whom God has taken out of Egypt to be God's own people.

First, though, the story focuses on the Egyptians, and on Pharaoh's claim that he does not know the Lord. When God tells Moses that he must go to Pharaoh again and that Pharaoh will listen to him only after God sends great signs and marvels, the charge concludes with: "And Egypt *will know* that I am the Lord, when I stretch out my hand over Egypt and bring out the Children of Israel from their midst" (7:5). If Pharaoh denies knowledge of the Lord now, and so refuses to send Israel, the eventual freeing of the Israelites will coincide with the Egyptians' coming to know that the one who demands their release is the Lord.

In fact, the ten plagues are structured around a progressive coming to know the Lord. As scholars have shown, the plagues are organized in three groups of three, plus the final plague—a structure that is reflected in the acronym recited in the Passover Haggadah: *detza"kh, ada"sh, be'aha"v*. Each of the sets of three plagues is heralded with Moses being sent to Pharaoh in the morning and announcing that God will send a plague. The first plague, blood, is introduced with: "By this you *will know* that I am Y-H-V-H" (7:17). The fourth plague, *arov*, is the first in which there will be a distinction between the land where the Israelites dwell and the rest of Egypt; the plague will affect the Egyptians but not the Israelites. Moses is to explain this to Pharaoh, saying "so that you *will know* that I am Y-H-V-H in the midst of the land" (8:18). The seventh plague, hail, which will be rained down in an astonishing display of God's might and wrath, will be sent "in order that you *will know* that there is none like me in all the land" (9:14; see also 9:29). The stated purpose of the plagues, time after time, is to counter Pharaoh's claim that he does not know the Lord and to force the response that knowledge of the Lord calls for. And, finally, at the splitting of the Sea, all of Egypt *"will know* that I am the Lord" (14:18).

The story of the plagues and the Exodus from Egypt, then, is focused on the Egyptians' coming to know the Lord. After the splitting of the Sea, the book turns its attention to the Israelites and to the fact that *they* have not known the Lord. This process of coming to know will be more complex and will take place in several stages over the course of the narrative of Exodus.

In the Song of the Sea, the Israelites declare: "Y-H-V-H is a man of war; Y-H-V-H is his name" (15:3). The Israelites' knowledge of God's name is striking; at the burning bush Moses had anticipated that the Israelites would inquire as to the name of the one who sent him and, after Moses's first mission to Pharaoh God had told Moses that God had not been known by the patriarchs by the name Y-H-V-H. Now the Israelites are able to proclaim God's identity as Y-H-V-H and, celebrating God's battle against the Egyptians, they understand Y-H-V-H to be a man of war.

Later in the Song, the Israelites go further: "Who is like you (*khamokhah*) among the gods, Y-H-V-H?!" (15:11). These two statements— the identification of God as Y-H-V-H and the acknowledgement that there is no one like Y-H-V-H—correspond to two of the three goals articulated by Moses to Pharaoh at the beginning of each set of three plagues: "by this you *will know* that I am Y-H-V-H" and "in order that you *will know* that there is none like me (*kamoni*) in all the land." The Israelites now know what they did not know before—and what the Egyptians had to come to know. But this correspondence highlights the missing third element: the Egyptians were also to come to know "that I am Y-H-V-H in the midst of (*be-kerev*) the land." Do the Israelites now know this as well?

While the Song explicitly mentions God's name and God's incomparability, it does not include the term *be-kerev*. It may be that there is an allusion to God's presence in the anticipation of building God's sanctuary: "You will bring them and plant them in the mountain of your inheritance, the place which you have made for your dwelling, Y-H-V-H, the sanctuary, my lord, that your hands have established" (15:17). But there is no explicit reference to God's presence *in the midst* of the land, or in the midst of the people as they journey through the wilderness.

In fact, not long after crossing the Sea, the people articulate their uncertainty about God's presence. The people come to Refidim and find no water there (17:1). On God's instruction, Moses strikes the rock with the staff that he had used to strike the Nile, and water flows from the rock (17:5-6). The episode culminates with the naming of the place after the people's quarrel and "their testing of the Lord, saying: 'Is Y-H-V-H in our midst (*be-kirbeinu*) or not?'" (17:7). "In the midst of the land" and "in our midst" may not signify precisely the same thing, but both terms refer to the Lord's presence and active engagement in earthly affairs. The absence of the term *be-kerev* in the Song, then, points toward something that the people do not know: Is the Lord present in their midst? As it turns out, the question of God's presence in the midst of the people will become a critical issue in the remainder of the book of Exodus.

At the Exodus, then, the Israelites have just begun to articulate knowledge of God. What it means to know God—and to know God as being in the midst of the people—will unfold over the course of the rest of the book. And knowledge of God will intersect with other kinds of knowledge, in particular with knowledge of how to walk compassionately in God's ways. Three passages in the second part of the book of Exodus—the story of Jethro's visit to Moses, the instructions for building the *mishkan*, and the conversation between Moses and God in the aftermath of the sin of the Golden Calf—elaborate the relationship between knowledge, intimacy with God, and compassionate action.

THE WAY IN WHICH THEY SHOULD WALK

After the Israelites' battle against Amalek, which immediately follows the Refidim story, Jethro comes to visit Moses, having heard of the Lord's redemption of Israel from Egypt (18:1-5). Moses tells his father-in-law what the Lord did to Pharaoh and the Egyptians, and also about the travails that the Israelites have encountered on their way, from which the Lord has saved them (18:8). Jethro rejoices and blesses the Lord "who has saved (*hitzil*) you," concluding, "Now I know that Y-H-V-H is greater than all gods…" (18:10-11). What Jethro knows is similar to what Pharaoh was to learn from the seventh plague and what the Israelites declared in the Song of the Sea: the Lord's incomparability to other gods. But the basis of Jethro's statement is different. The words *va-yatzileim* and *hitzil* occur several times in the interchange between Moses and his father-in-law.

To Know and Be Known

What evokes Jethro's blessing of the Lord and his declaration of the Lord's incomparable greatness is the knowledge that Y-H-V-H is a God who saves.

This same quality of saving someone from their oppressor is what brought Jethro close to Moses in the first place. When the young Moses fled from Egypt to Midian and helped Jethro's daughters, who had been chased away by the shepherds, the young women told their father "an Egyptian man saved us (*hitzilanu*) from the shepherds..." (2:15-19). Jethro insisted that his daughters invite the man to come and share a meal, and Moses stayed with Jethro, who gave him his daughter Zipporah as a wife (2:20-21). Now, bringing Zipporah back to Moses (18:2), Jethro rejoices about this very quality of saving that he learns characterizes Y-H-V-H.

Jethro's knowledge, then, relates to a moral quality—the Lord is great not only because the Lord does great wonders but because the Lord saves. As we saw earlier, God revealed to Moses God's plan to save Israel (*lehatzilo*) at the burning bush, in consequence of God's knowledge of their sufferings (3:7-8). The story of that revelation appears immediately after Moses saves Jethro's daughters. So the Lord's quality of saving is reflected in Moses's act of saving, both are appreciated by Jethro, and both are linked to knowledge: the Lord's saving emerging from his knowledge of the people's suffering, and Jethro's knowledge of the Lord's incommensurable greatness emerging from his recognition of the Lord's saving.

The theme of knowledge reappears in this story shortly after. The day after his arrival, Jethro sees Moses sitting in judgment and the people standing before him all day. Jethro questions why Moses is sitting alone— "*madu'a* (why?—an interrogative based on the root meaning "to know") *atah yosheiv levadekha*"—with all the people standing before him. Moses replies that the people come to seek God; when they have a dispute, they come before him for judgment, "and I *make known* to them God's statutes and instructions." Jethro replies: "The thing that you are doing is not good" (18:14-17). Moses cannot do this alone, Jethro warns. Moses should appoint others who can judge the people, leaving only the difficult cases to Moses himself. His main task should be to bring the people's cases before God, to "charge them with the statutes and instructions," and to "*make known* to them the way in which they should walk and the deed that they should do" (18:18-20).

How precisely we might understand Moses's and Jethro's conceptions of Moses's task is a matter of interpretation on which commentators

83

differ. But it is clear that, besides suggesting that Moses appoint people who can share the task of judging the people, Jethro construes Moses's responsibilities somewhat differently than Moses himself does. While Moses and Jethro both talk of things that Moses must make known to the people, what it is that each says must be made known is different. Moses uses "to make known" in relation to the statutes and instructions. Jethro agrees that Moses should charge the people with these things, but he reserves "to make known" for the additional element that he adds: "the way in which they should walk and the deed that they should do."

What are the way and the deed that Moses needs to make known to the people? Given the distinction between these things and "the statutes and instructions," I think that the way and the deed are not rules to follow but rather ways of walking and acting in the world that are not reducible to rules. This understanding is reflected in a tannaitic *midrash*:

> "And you will make known to them
> the way in which they should walk"—this is Torah study;
> "and the deed that they should do"—this is the good deed
> —the words of Rabbi Yehoshua.
>
> Rabbi Elazar ha-Moda'i says—
> "And you will make known to them"—
> make known to them their means of livelihood;
> "the way"—this is visiting the sick;
> "they should walk"—this is burying the dead;
> "in which"—this is doing acts of kindness;
> "and the deed"—this is what is required by law;
> "that they should do"—
> this is going beyond what is required by law
> (*lifnim mi-shurat ha-din*).
>
> *Mekhilta de-Rabbi Yishmael, Yitro Amalek 2*

The two sages in this passage offer different elaborations of the words and phrases that constitute Jethro's description of what Moses is to make known to the people. But both sages point to things that are not spelled out by rules, things that go beyond the requirements of the law, that are acts of kindness between a person and their fellow. Jethro, then, is saying to Moses that, while he must instruct the people in the law, he must also help them come to know something else. Knowledge, for Jethro, is a kind of moral sensibility, a path that a person must learn to walk and a way of behaving that a person must learn to navigate. The people must come to internalize an aspiration toward ethical behavior that goes beyond the laws in which they are instructed. It is this that Jethro describes as knowledge.

This sensibility is akin to the kind of knowing that both Moses's sister and God manifested early in the book: empathic understanding of the experience of the other that leads to taking responsibility for helping the one who is in need. This kind of knowing, and the responsibilities that it entails, complements law. It also serves as the foundation for one of the laws that Moses is to lay before the people in Parashat Mishpatim. Mishpatim closely follows the story of Jethro's visit. That visit—and the people's desire to seek God and and God's instruction (18:15-16)—anticipates the revelation at Sinai (chs. 19-20) in Parashat Yitro and God's spelling out to Moses the laws that he is to set out before the people (chs. 21-23) in Parashat Mishpatim. The laws of Mishpatim are many and varied, but (as Ibn Ezra notes in his short commentary on 21:1) overall there is an emphasis on how those who are marginal or downtrodden are to be treated. In fact, Mishpatim begins with the laws of male and female slaves (21:2-11), taking as its point of departure a condition from which the Israelites have just emerged and implicitly appealing to their experience in asking them to treat their own slaves differently. An explicit appeal to the Israelites' experience and their capacity and responsibility to have empathy for those who are suffering comes later in this corpus of laws: "You shall not oppress the stranger, for *you know* the soul of a stranger, for you were strangers in the land of Egypt" (23:9).

Unlike the laws about slaves, which are detailed in a way that can be operationalized, the law about oppressing the stranger is a fuzzy law. God does not spell out *how* the stranger is not to be oppressed; instead there is an appeal to the Israelites' understanding of the experience of the stranger and the moral imperative that derives from that kind of understanding.

In fact, the prohibition against oppressing the stranger had already been articulated several verses earlier, along with a prohibition against mistreating widows and orphans:

> [20]A stranger you shall not mistreat,
> and you shall not oppress him,
> because you were strangers in the land of Egypt.

²¹Any widow or orphan you shall not afflict.
²²If you indeed afflict him, if he then indeed cries out to me,
I will indeed hear his cry.
²³And my anger will be kindled, and I will kill you by sword,
and your wives will be widows and your children orphans.

Exodus 22:20-23

This passage is remarkable in several ways. First, a reason is given for the first prohibition: you may not oppress the stranger, "*because* you were strangers." Further, a consequence is stated for violating the law: "I will kill you by sword." The articulation of this consequence seems designed not only to deter disobedience in order to avoid punishment but to teach a lesson: "your wives will be widows and your children orphans." The formulation seems intended to evoke the kind of empathy that the person who might think of abusing the widow and orphan lacks; your family, too, could be marginalized and abused. Both the prohibition against oppressing the stranger and the prohibition against afflicting the widow and orphan appeal to the experience of the person who is being commanded—either to an experience that they have actually had or to an experience that they are asked to imagine. Here, as in the later passage, memory or imagination of a personal experience is to be the basis of empathy, and empathy is to be the basis of moral responsibility—which, here, is articulated in a divine command.

Yet another noteworthy feature of this passage is the emphatic nature of the verbs. Verse 22 contains three verbs in a double formulation (infinitive absolute plus imperfect), translated above each time with the addition of the word "indeed": "*aneih te'aneh*"; "*tza'ok yitz'ak*"; "*shamo'a eshma*." There is a sense of egregiousness and of urgency: the outrageous oppression of the stranger will provoke an anguished outcry, which will prompt a deep and responsive hearing. The crying out of the oppressed and God's hearing of the cry recall God's response to the Israelites' enslavement at the end of chapter 2. There, God heard and God knew, leading God to call on Moses to be God's instrument in saving the people from oppression. Here, the description of God's outrage at the possibility of an Israelite oppressing a stranger or widow or orphan has the effect of inviting the Israelites' own moral outrage at the possibility of behaving in the way that *their* oppressors had. *You* know what it means to be oppressed, God is saying; if you don't, then imagine what it would be like for your own family to be marginalized and oppressed; and if you can't, then I will intervene with the same wrath that I poured onto the Egyptians when they oppressed you.

Taken together, these two passages about treatment of a stranger highlight two elements of what it means not only to be informed of God's commandments but to know the path on which to walk and the deed that must be done. The Israelites are invited to dig into their own experience and behave with empathic responsibility toward others. God commands caring behavior toward the stranger, but the command is articulated in relation to the people's internal capacity for moral discernment. In addition, as noted, this set of prohibitions is left fuzzy. Based as these commands are in experience and empathy, the people are asked to know what it means to be a stranger or widow or orphan and to know, from the insight gained from their own experience, how they are to act in relation to those who are suffering.

TO DWELL IN THEIR MIDST

After God communicates the laws that Moses is to set before the people and formalizes the covenant whose terms those laws constitute (24:3-8), God commands the Israelites to gather materials to build a sanctuary (25:1-7). The purpose and function of the *mishkan* and its furnishings is stated several times. The first such statement appears right after a listing of the materials that are to be gathered, when God informs Moses of the project for which the materials will be used and of the purpose of that project: "And they will make for me a sanctuary, that I may dwell (*ve-shakhanti*) in their midst (*be-tokham*)" (25:8).

This purpose is striking in the context of the Israelites' earlier wondering whether the Lord is in their midst (*be-kirbeinu*). The words for "in the midst" used in the two passages are different and may have different resonances. But, as we will see, the earlier word—*be-kirbeinu*—will be used again later in the book, and that usage will relate to the Lord's presence among the people as reified in the *mishkan*. So, as God introduces the plan to build a sanctuary, anticipated by the Israelites in the Song of the Sea (15:17), God asserts something that had been omitted in the Song and that the Israelites, it turned out, were not sure of as they left Egypt and began their wanderings in the wilderness. God asserts that God will be present in the midst of the people. God's presence "in the midst of," as we saw, was one of the things that the Egyptians were to come to know by means of the plagues, and so the Israelites' uncertainty about God's presence indicated a lack of knowledge, in contrast to their having come to know Y-H-V-H's identity and incommensurability. God's instructions now to build a sanctuary so that the Lord can dwell in the midst of the people fills out the knowledge that the Israelites have been progressively attaining.

As instructions for the construction of the *mishkan*, the priestly garments, and the inauguration of the priests into divine service draw to a conclusion, awareness of God's presence is explicitly described as *knowledge*: "And I will dwell in the midst of the Children of Israel, and I will be their God. And they *will know* that I am Y-H-V-H their God who took them out of the land of Egypt to dwell in their midst. I am Y-H-V-H their God" (29:45-46). When the Israelites were still in Egypt, God had told Moses to relay his promise to deliver them from their enslavement "and you *will know* that I am Y-H-V-H your God who took you out from under the burdens of Egypt" (6:7). Now, with the building of the *mishkan*, the Israelites will not just know that Y-H-V-H is the one who delivered them; they will know that Y-H-V-H dwells in their midst—indeed, that Y-H-V-H delivered them *in order to* dwell in their midst.

What it means for the Lord to dwell in the midst of the people is also spelled out here. The *mishkan*, also called the Tent of Meeting (*ohel mo'eid*), is the place in which "I will meet (*iva'eid*) with you there to speak to you there. And I will meet (*ve-no'adeti*) there with the Children of Israel, and they will be sanctified by my glory" (29:42-43). The Hebrew root meaning "to meet" or "to encounter"—*y-'-d*—is an anagram of the root meaning "to know"—*y-d-'*. The Lord's dwelling in the midst of the people means that the people will be able to encounter the Lord.

A third similar root—*'-v-d*—appeared immediately before, in the description of the ark and its cover, the *kaporet*. God instructs Moses to place the *kaporet* over the ark and to put into the ark the *'edut* (25:21). The word *'edut* is a signifier for the tablets (the two words are combined in 32:15), connoting the tablets' function as a sign of the covenant. "And I will meet (*ve-no'adeti*) with you there, and I will speak to you from above the *kaporet* from between the two cherubs that are on the ark of the *'edut* all that I will command you to the Children of Israel" (25:22). The Lord's dwelling place, then, is a place of encounter and also a place of instruction.

The covenantal revelation and instruction in the laws that began at Sinai will continue in the *mishkan*, as Ramban points out in his introduction to Parashat Terumah.

The plays on the root *y-d-'* in the instructions for the *mishkan*, then, extend the notion of knowledge. The *mishkan* enables the people to know that God dwells in their midst, and it is also the place in which the people will continue to gain knowledge of God's way, as God will dispense instruction from between the cherubs who are above the ark that contains the tablets of the covenant. (In fact, the very first mention of the tablets, at the culmination of the covenant ceremony in Exodus 24, juxtaposes the tablets and God's instruction: "I will give you the tablets of stone and the *torah* and the *mitzvah* that I have written to instruct them" [24:12].)

That the *mishkan* is a site of knowledge and that instruction is accessible from between the cherubs is striking, because in Genesis, after the first humans had eaten from the forbidden Tree of Knowledge and been expelled from Eden, God had stationed the cherubs east of Eden to block the way back to the Garden. In the *mishkan*, too, the cherubs appear on the curtains (26:1) and on the partition that is placed before the ark (26:31-34)—but the divine voice breaks through those divisions to continue to bring God's command to the people. While in the Garden, then, the presence of the cherubs is the consequence of illegitimately achieving knowledge, in the *mishkan* the cherubs' demarcation of the site of the divine presence both signifies the boundaries of human reach and affords access to divinely granted expansion of knowledge.

In fact, the *mishkan* is built *through* knowledge. Bezalel is appointed by God to oversee the construction of the sanctuary and its appurtenances: "And I have filled him with the spirit of God, with wisdom and with understanding and with *knowledge* and with all [manner of] work[manship]..." (Exodus 31:2-3). All those who participate in the work also are described as having the wisdom and understanding *to know* (36:1). Construction of the *mishkan*, then, is the creation *through* knowledge of a world *whose purpose* is knowledge.

Modern scholars as well as classical *midrashim* have pointed out the many parallels between the construction of the *mishkan* and the creation stories of Genesis. In fact, the entire narrative from the beginning of Genesis through the end of Exodus is framed by these two world-creating acts. The *mishkan's* construction is a response to the loss of Eden, restoring the possibility of living with the presence of God. And it is the culmination of the human being's search for knowledge, establishing the proper place of human knowledge in relation to God. Both of these themes are evoked in the *mishkan*-related passages about knowledge. And Bezalel's ability to do the work (*melakhah*)—resonating with the thrice-mentioned *melakhah* at the culmination of the creation story (Genesis 2:2-3)—is enabled by the "spirit of God" with which he is filled—echoing the *ruaḥ elohim* that hovers over the waters at the inception of the creation story (1:2).

The word *tokh*, used in the *mishkan* passage for God's presence in the midst of the people, is a marked word in the Eden story, used three times in reference to the Trees of Life and of Knowledge and the trees amongst which Adam and Eve hide after eating the forbidden fruit (2:9; 3:3, 8). The use of the word *tokh* in the *mishkan* passage, in place of the word *kerev* used elsewhere in Exodus in reference to God's presence among the people, evokes the Eden narrative. The word will appear again in a passage at the end of Leviticus that describes how the people will live if they obey God's command, offering a vision that conflates Eden and the *mishkan* (Leviticus 26:3-13). The description concludes: "And I will set my dwelling (*mishkani*) in your midst (*be-tokhakhem*)... and I will walk (*ve-hithalakhti*) in your midst (*be-tokhakhem*)" (26:11-12). The intensive form of the word "walk" recalls the Lord's walking about (*mithalekh*) in the Garden of Eden, as Adam and his wife hide amidst (*be-tokh*) the trees of the Garden (Genesis 3:8). God's presence *be-tokh* the people in this Leviticus passage evokes the Eden story as it portrays what it would be like for God to place God's dwelling amidst the people. The use of *tokh* in the *mishkan* passage, is a subtle evocation of a place in which people once lived in God's presence, a place from which human beings were banished after gaining knowledge, but that God now charges them to reconstruct, in a transmuted form, through knowledge.

Looking back at the Jethro passage, it is noteworthy that a number of elements of that story as well recall elements of the creation story. In particular, Jethro asks Moses why he is sitting "alone (*levadekha*)" (Exodus 18:14). And, after Moses explains the nature of his work, Jethro replies: "the thing that you are doing is not good (*lo tov*)" (18:16). The combination of "not good" and "alone" recalls the creation of the human being in Genesis 2. After a chapter in which God repeatedly sees that things are good, and after the word *tov* reappears in the description of one of the lands fed by the tributaries of Eden's river (Genesis 2:12), we suddenly hear a jarring *lo tov*—"It is *not good* for the human being to be alone (*levado*)" (2:18).

To Know and Be Known

Of course, the Genesis passage has already foregrounded the idea of an alternative to *tov*, as God plants the Tree of Knowledge of Good and Evil (2:9) and forbids the human being to eat of its fruit (2:17). It is immediately after issuing this prohibition that God asserts that it is not good for the human being to be alone, and articulates a plan to fill the human need for a companion who can help him (2:18). Thus, the complexities of human knowledge are intertwined with the need for human companionship, and both are linked to the valence of good or its opposite. This same cluster of issues occurs in the Jethro passage, as the quest for knowledge and Moses's need to make things known evoke an evaluation that it is not good for Moses to be alone and a plan to provide Moses with companions to help in the work.

The questions of the proper way to access knowledge and the necessary kinds of knowledge to be sought, then, rise to the surface already in the Jethro passage. The *mishkan* passage continues this trajectory, focusing on the critical issue of using knowledge to enable God to dwell in the midst of the people. And the relationship between knowledge and the ability of God to be with the people will be central to the conversation between Moses and God in the aftermath of the sin of the Golden Calf.

KNOWING GOD'S WAYS

The long series of chapters that lay out the plan for the *mishkan* and that describe the process of its construction are interrupted by the story of the Golden Calf. While Moses is on the mountain receiving God's instructions, the people demand that Aaron make a god for them, and they proclaim the calf that he makes to be the god who took them out of Egypt (Exodus 32:1-4). God threatens to destroy the people, but Moses prays for a change of heart, and God accedes to Moses's plea not to destroy them (32:9-14).

Much later in the story, Moses speaks to God again: "See, you say to me 'bring up this people,' but you *have not made known* to me whom you will send with me. Yet you said to me 'I *have known* you by name and you have found favor in my eyes'" (33:12). This verse initiates an extended interchange between Moses and God, in which the verb "to know" appears repeatedly. Preceding this interchange, God had instructed Moses to go up to the promised land along with the people and had told him that God will not go up in their midst—*be-kirbekha*—but will, instead, send an angel before the people (33:1-3). The people mourn when they hear this bad news, and they refrain from adorning themselves (33:4). God is prompted to explain God's decision not to accompany them: "You are a stiff-necked people; if I were to go up in your midst for a moment, I would destroy you. Now take off your adornments, and I *will know* what I will do to/for you" (33:5). "So," concludes this episode, "the Children of Israel stripped themselves of their adornments from Mount Horeb" (33:6).

While God has resolved not to destroy the people for their sin, there has been a significant change of plan. God refuses to go in the midst of the people. The people mourn at the news of this loss of God's presence, which leads God to inform them that this is for their own good—if God were to accompany them, they would be in danger of destruction because of their propensity to sin again. The angel that God will send instead will enable the people to take possession of the promised land but will be less of a threat to the stiff-necked people. At the end of this initial interchange, God seems willing to reconsider: God "will know" what to do, but meanwhile the people must remove their adornments.

In fact, the removal of adornments is mentioned three times in this passage, in three consecutive verses, and it seems to be intimately related to God's reconsideration of God's refusal to accompany the people. Notably, the word for adornments consists of the letters ʿ, *d*, and *y*, the letters of the root *y-d-ʿ*—"to know"—in reverse order. The word also recalls the other words in the *mishkan* passage that echoed "to know," *y-ʿ-d* ("to meet" or "to encounter"), and *ʿ-v-d*, referring to the tablets of the covenant. Now those tablets have been broken and the plan to construct the *mishkan*— the place of encounter with God—has, apparently, been suspended, for God's refusal to be in the midst of the people means that there will be no *mishkan*. The people's mourning, expressed in the removal of their adornments, is a reflection of the loss of this presence, the rupture of the covenant, and the interruption to their access to the knowledge of God that the *mishkan* was to enable.

Forms of "to know" itself appear seven times in the extended conversation between God and Moses that begins with God's instruction to Moses to bring the people to the land without God's accompaniment. The first occurs when God promises to reconsider God's decision not to accompany the people. The rest appear one after the other as Moses launches an appeal to God that, step by step, leads to God consenting to be in the midst of the people.

At first, Moses does not explicitly ask God to accompany the people. Instead, he says that God has not *made known* to him whom God will send, yet God has said "I *know* you by name and you have found favor (*hein*) in my eyes" (33:12). Moses continues, "And now, if I have found favor (*hein*) in your eyes, *let me know* your ways that I may *know* you, in order that I may find favor (*hein*) in your eyes. And see that this nation is your people" (33:13).

What does Moses mean when he asserts that God has said "I know you by name," and how is this related to Moses's request to know God and God's ways? One possibility is that "I know you by name" means that God has singled out Moses, calling him by name and choosing him to be in special relationship with God. If God and Moses are intimates, Moses says, then Moses desires deeper knowledge of God: "Let me know your ways that I may know you."

At the same time, the word "name" along with the verb "to know" recalls God's notice to Moses early in the Exodus narrative that God had not made Godself known to the patriarchs by the name Y-H-V-H. Moses was to tell the Israelites God's identity as Y-H-V-H, and relate to them God's promise to redeem them and to bring them to the promised land (6:2-8). "I know you by name" might be alluding to that promise, suggesting not only that God has singled out Moses by *Moses's* name but that God knows Moses by means of *God's* name—that the special relationship between God and Moses is expressed in God's new manifestation as Y-H-V-H. If so, then Moses is saying: "You said that you will relate to me and the people by making your name known—but then I need to know you." Moses, then, is asking for an enhanced revelation of God's essence. God had made it clear that no one has ever really known who God is; Moses is now pleading for that knowledge: "Let me know your ways that I may know you."

Knowing the way recalls Jethro telling Moses that he is to make known to the people the way in which they should walk (18:20). Accordingly, as suggested by Maimonides's interpretation of this passage (Guide for the Perplexed 1:54), Moses may be asking God to let Moses know God's ways as a model for the ways in which Moses himself is to walk as he leads the people. Alternatively, Moses may be asking God to make known to Moses the ways in which *God* must walk if God is to be with the people. Strikingly, God responds to Moses's request by saying: "My presence will go, and I will give you rest" (33:14). And Moses replies: "If your presence does not go, do not bring us up from here! For by what shall it *be known* that I have found favor (*hein*) in your eyes—I and your people—is it not by means of your going with us…?" (33:15-16). God has understood Moses's request to know God's ways, then, as a request that God accompany the people. Moses's repeated reference to finding favor—*hein*—in God's eyes is responded to by God's promise to go with the people and to give them rest—*ve-hani*ḥ*oti*, playing on the word for favor.

At stake in this extended conversation, then, is God's ability to be present among the people. This capacity, it turns out, is a function of the divine qualities of grace (*hein*) and compassion. When Moses requests knowledge of God, he is told that God will call out "in the name of Y-H-V-H" (33:19). And, indeed, after Moses carves out new stone tablets, replacing the tablets of the broken covenant, God calls out what is known in Jewish tradition as the thirteen attributes of mercy (34:6-7). God calling out God's name means that God is defining Godself; God is offering an elaboration or interpretation of the divine name Y-H-V-H. While in chapter 3, God had self-identified with the oblique *ehyeh asher ehyeh* ("I will be that I will be"), and in chapter 6, God had said that God will manifest to the people as Y-H-V-H, now God spells out who Y-H-V-H is: "Y-H-V-H, a god who is compassionate and gracious (*ḥanun*)" (33:6).

Moses's request to know God's ways, then, is not a request for a general knowledge of God. Rather, Moses is saying: Let me know your ways that will enable you to walk with us. The self-definition that God offers in response is a particular manifestation of God—a way of God's being in the world—that will enable God to go with the people. In fact, in response to God's spelling out of God's name, Moses says something astonishing: "If I have found favor (*hein*) in your eyes, let the Lord go in the midst of us, for it is a stiff-necked people, and you will forgive our iniquities and our sins…" (34:9). Earlier, God had said that God could *not* go in the midst of the people precisely because they are a stiff-necked people; when they sin, as they are bound to do, God would destroy them (33:3). But now Moses asks God to go in the midst of the people *because* they are a stiff-necked people. God, and God alone, Moses is suggesting, has the capacity to forgive the people, and that is why it must be God who accompanies the people. It is the way in which God has now chosen to make Godself known, the way God has defined the name Y-H-V-H, that will enable God to do this.

To Know and Be Known

Exodus—*Sefer Shemot*, the Book of Names—begins with a list of the sons of Jacob, the children of Israel. The book soon moves on to anonymity, as the Israelites multiply in swarms and as even Moses's father, mother, and sister are introduced without names. Later, individuals such as Moses are given names, and the architect of the *mishkan*, Bezalel, is "called by name" (31:2). The naming of God fits within this theme of namelessness and having a name.

But whether God's name denotes who God is is not clear. When Moses first asks who he should tell the people has sent him, God replies, *"ehyeh asher ehyeh,"* instructing Moses to tell the people *"ehyeh* sent me to you" (3:14). *Ehyeh*, of course, is the first-person form of Y-H-V-H, the name by which God asks Moses to introduce Godself to the people in the following verse. But what does that identification signify? "I/he will be" might mean that God will manifest however God manifests; there is no way to pin down God's identity. Alternatively, it might suggest presence, God's assurance that God will be with Moses (*ki ehyeh imakh*, 3:12). But in the aftermath of the sin of the Golden Calf, the episode that threatens the plan for God to dwell in the midst of the people, the divine name gains specific content. For the first time, God defines Godself, and this self-definition is in the service of God's ability not only to be with Moses but to walk in the midst of the people.

Knowing God's name, then, has to do with coming into a relationship. That, I think, is the significance of the odd construction of the phrase with which God had told Moses that God had not manifested to the patriarchs as Y-H-V-H: *"u-shmi y-h-v-h lo noda'ti lahem."* God is not simply saying that God didn't inform the patriarchs of the name Y-H-V-H, nor is God just saying that God didn't manifest to them as Y-H-V-H. What God seems to be saying is: "I was not made known to them in a way that would let them know who I am"—in other words, the kind of knowledge that the patriarchs did not have, which Moses is told *will* be given to the Israelites, is knowledge that can only be gained through a particular kind of experience. The Israelites come to know God's name as they come to know God and as God chooses to make known those ways of being that enable God to be with the people.

And so if, in the beginning of the book, there was a lack in the people's knowledge of God, there was also a lack in the way God manifested Godself. Knowing, as we have seen, is a moral imperative. Once Adam and Eve partake of the fruit of the Tree of Knowledge, human beings cannot escape from the imperative to know. Thereafter, to say "I do not know," to choose not to know, is problematic. In the book of Exodus, the people do not know God, but God also has not made Godself known. Knowledge becomes a *relational* moral imperative. God makes Godself known by choosing to walk in a certain way; in fact, it is the way in which God chooses to walk that God makes known in the spelling out of God's name. And knowing God's ways becomes an imperative for the people, who need to know "the way in which they should walk." This reciprocal knowing of the way—God's knowing how God can walk with the people and the people's knowing how they can walk with God—requires an alignment of paths that is the challenge of the book of Exodus, a book that culminates with the community of Israel building a sanctuary in which God can be present in their midst.

PRAYING FOR COMPASSION

In a striking talmudic passage, God is portrayed as praying. What, asks the Talmud, does God pray?

> "May it be my will that my compassion vanquish my anger
> and that my compassion overwhelm my attributes
> and that I conduct myself toward my children
> with the attribute of compassion
> and that I go for them beyond what is required by law
> (*lifnim mi-shurat ha-din*)."

The Talmud repeats this prayer as the words of the High Priest Rabbi Yishmael, when he entered into the Holy of Holies and was asked by God for a blessing:

> I said to him:
> "May it be your will that your compassion vanquish your anger
> and that your compassion overwhelm your attributes
> and that you conduct yourself toward your children
> with the attribute of compassion
> and that you go for them beyond what is required by law."
> And he nodded his head to me.

Bavli Berakhot 7a

God needs to pray—to Godself!—that the divine attribute of compassion be activated toward Israel. And God needs the blessing of the High Priest—Israel's human representative—that God be able to foreground the divine attribute of compassion.

It's not so simple, the passage seems to be saying, for God to act with compassion. There are competing attributes through which God might manifest in the world. To act with compassion is a choice, and it is a difficult one, one that needs constant reminders, encouragement, and support.

The passage recalls the conversation between Moses and God in the aftermath of the sin of the Golden Calf. God has not always revealed Godself as a compassionate God. God has warned Moses that it is dangerous for God to be present with the people, because the people will inevitably fail to be loyal to God, and God will become enraged and destroy them. But Moses refuses to lose the intimacy and directness of the relationship with God. He appeals to God to show him God's ways, to let him *know* God. And God, finally, reaches into the complex divine self and discloses to Moses the range of attributes through which God can manifest in the world. In this process, God prioritizes the attributes of compassion and grace—*rahum ve-hanun*. And Moses understands that God has acceded to his request to find a way to go with the people, to be present in their midst despite their failings.

In both God's prayer and the High Priest's blessing, the aspiration of compassion appears three times, underscoring the challenge of activating compassion among competing drives and in response to behavior that can rupture and destroy relationship. But there is a fourth element in the prayer and the blessing: "that I/you go for them beyond what is required by law (*lifnim mi-shurat ha-din*)." That God aspires to act *lifnim mi-shurat ha-din*—that the attribute of compassion that God reveals in response to Moses's request *to know God's ways* goes hand in hand with going beyond what is required by law—recalls the *midrash* on Jethro's advice to Moses. Beyond instructing the people in the statutes, Jethro tells his son-in-law, Moses must *make known* to the people "the way in which they walk and the deed that they should do." According to the *midrash*, this refers to acts of compassion, to what the law requires as well as to how the people should go beyond what is required by law—*lifnim mi-shurat ha-din*.

The *midrash* on Jethro's advice and the talmudic passage about God's prayer and the High Priest's blessing both imagine what it might mean to truly know or become known. What is the way that the people must come to know, and what are God's ways that Moses seeks to know and that God Godself must continuously strive to make known in the world? The people who have been redeemed from enslavement to become God's people must come to know the way of empathy and compassionate behavior, going beyond what is required to do what is needed. And God makes known—and, according to the talmudic passage, struggles to continue to make known—the attributes of compassion and grace, forgiving his people so that he can walk in their midst and inspire them toward walking in the way of compassionate knowing and doing.

GOD'S ETERNAL ENEMY

> The Blessed Holy One swears
> that his name is not complete
> and his throne is not complete
> until the name of Amalek will be entirely blotted out....
>
> *Rashi on Exodus 17:16*

WHAT IS AMALEK? How might we understand the nature of this enemy that comes to attack Israel as the newly redeemed people are on their way, tired and weary, to the promised land? What is it about Amalek that leads Rashi, and the *midrash* that he cites, to assign Amalek a cosmic role in relation to God's dominion? Who is this enemy that, the Torah enjoins us, we are to remember always and seek to obliterate (Deuteronomy 25:17-19)?

Amalek attacks Israel when the people are "tired and weary" (25:18), and so one way of understanding Amalek and its attack on Israel is to focus on Israel's weakness—Amalek can be seen as an externalization of Israel's weakness or as an entity that discloses Israel's unworthiness. Alternatively, Amalek can see be seen, as in the *midrash* that Rashi cites, as an enemy not only of Israel, but of God—Amalek's existence makes impossible a world in which God has complete dominion, in which God's name and God's throne, in Rashi's words, can be complete. It is this second understanding of Amalek that will be the focus of this essay, but I want to begin by illustrating the contrasting perspective, the idea that Amalek's attack discloses a deep weakness in Israel itself.

"YOU WERE TIRED AND WEARY"

Amalek comes to battle with Israel at the moment that the Israelites have expressed doubt as to whether God's presence is among them. "Is the Lord in our midst or not?" they ask (Exodus 17:7). "And Amalek came" (17:8).

Midrashim on this episode highlight Israel's weakness. The place where this battle transpires is called Refidim (17:8)—midrashically explicated as *rifyon yadayim*, "weakness of hands" (Mekhilta de-Rabbi Yishmael BeShallah Amalek 1). Rashi cites a *midrash* that illustrates the juxtaposition of Israel's question about God's presence with the encounter with Amalek: It is like a father who carries his little child on his shoulders wherever he goes. Whatever the child sees and asks for, the father gives him. But then the child sees a passerby and asks him: "Have you seen father?" The father says: "You don't know where I am?!" He sets the child down, and the child is bitten by a dog (Rashi on Exodus 17:8). It is the Israelites' inability to recognize the presence and protection of God, this *midrash* is suggesting, that is expressed in their vulnerability to Amalek. God has redeemed Israel from Egyptian enslavement, but Israel is not fully worthy of redemption, of crossing over from enslavement to the promised land, of becoming God's people.

A similar way of seeing Amalek is strikingly expressed in a Hasidic teaching told by Rabbi Shlomo Carlebach. When God created the world, God made a deal with the sea. "Many, many years from now," God said, "my people will come to your shore. They will be escaping from enslavement, and their oppressors will be chasing after them. When that happens, let your waters move aside, and make room for my people to pass through." "How will I know," asks the sea, "who is your people?" So God gives the sea a picture of God's people. "When *this* people comes to your shore," God says, "let them pass through." Many years later, the Israelites come to the shore of the sea. The sea looks at them, looks at the picture, looks at them again—the people standing on the shore do not look anything like the people in the picture, and the sea refuses to part. God needs to intervene. "This *is* my people," God explains, "but they have been worn down by years of exile and enslavement. The picture that I gave you is a picture of what they are really like. Let them pass through, and they will come to be like that." The sea parts. But then Amalek comes.

Amalek, according to this teaching, is that which tells you that you can never be different from how you are right now. Amalek is that which tells the sea that the people that it sees is what the people will forever be like. Amalek tells the people that, though the sea has parted for them, they will never become the people in the picture that God showed the sea at the beginning of time. Amalek is a manifestation of one's own vulnerability, of not knowing who you are or who you need to be, of not being able to change. Amalek is whatever is inside us that tries to keep us from crossing over into the promised land.

Amalek's enmity toward Israel can also be seen as a response to Jacob's violation of his brother Esau, Amalek's grandfather. Hizkuni suggests that Amalek battles against Israel because of the enduring hatred that Amalek harbors over Esau's selling of his birthright to Jacob (Hizkuni on Exodus 17:8). Remembering the story of Israel's and Amalek's ancestors invites us to consider Amalek's aggression as a consequence, wrong as it is, of Jacob/Israel's own actions. At the same time, the notion that Jacob/Israel's past wrong is never forgiven by Amalek returns us to Carlebach's point—that Amalek refuses to consider the possibility of transformation.

This idea that Amalek is a manifestation of our own weakness, our past failures, our inability to transform ourselves correlates with one of two possible readings of the verses in Deuteronomy that enjoin us to remember Amalek:

> ¹⁷Remember what Amalek did to you on the way,
> when you came out of Egypt.
> ¹⁸How he came upon you on the way
> and attacked those who were hindmost among you,
> and you were tired and weary,
> and *not fearing God*....
>
> *Deuteronomy 25:17-18*

Who is it that did not fear God? One way to read this phrase is as a continuation of the description of Israel: "You were tired and weary and not God-fearing" (reading *yerei*, an adjective, rather than *yarei*). According to this reading, *Israel* was not God-fearing; Israel was weak not only physically but in a spiritual sense. They were, as the *midrash* says, *rifei yadayim*, weak of hands, in their questioning of God, in their inability to truly cross over to be God's people. It is Israel's weakness, according to this reading, that is made manifest in Amalek's attack.

An alternative reading, reflected in both the traditional masoretic parsing (the word for "weary" is marked with an *etnaḥta*, signaling the main break in the verse) and vocalization (*yarei*—a verb in the third person), is that it is *Amalek* that did not fear God: "You were weak and weary, and *he* did not fear God." According to this reading, Amalek is an external enemy, an enemy who takes advantage of those who are weak and weary and most vulnerable ("those who were hindmost among you"), an enemy who does not fear God. It is this understanding of Amalek as an external enemy that I want to develop in the remainder of this essay.

"HE DID NOT FEAR GOD"

What could it mean that Amalek is an enemy who does not fear God?

The final verse of the story of Amalek in the book of Exodus contains an elliptical phrase:

> And he said:
> Because a hand is on the throne (*kes*) of the Lord (Y-H),
>   a war for the Lord against Amalek
>   from generation to generation.
>
> *Exodus 17:16*

Rashi understands the hand on the throne as signifying an oath: God swears on God's throne that God will be at war with Amalek for all eternity. Rashi continues by citing a stunning *midrash* that offers an explanation of the unusual rendering of the word for throne in this verse (*kes*, rather than *kisei*) as well as the short form of God's name (Y-H, rather than Y-H-V-H):

> "The Blessed Holy One swears
> that his name is not complete and his throne is not complete,
> until the name of Amalek will be entirely blotted out.
> And when his [Amalek's] name will be blotted out,
> the name [of God] will be complete and the throne complete,

as it says:
"The enemy has come to an end in everlasting ruins"—
this is Amalek... —
"you have uprooted their cities,
their very memory is destroyed" (Psalm 9:7).

What does it say after that?

"But the Lord (Y-H-V-H) will sit forever"—
behold, his name is complete—
"he has established his throne (*kis'o*) in justice" (Psalm 9:8)—
behold, his throne is complete.

God's dominion on earth, Rashi tells us, is not complete. Only once the enemy is destroyed—only when its memory is obliterated—will God manifest in the fullness of God's name and will God be completely enthroned. The *midrash* that Rashi cites picks up on the word "memory" in Psalm 9:7 ("their very memory is destroyed")—and also, no doubt, on the preceding verse's assertion that God has "blotted out" the name of the enemy (Psalm 9:6)—and links it with the same words and ideas in the Amalek story. After the battle with Amalek, God tells Moses "Write this as a memorial in a book... that I will utterly *blot out the memory/name* of Amalek from under the heavens" (Exodus 17:14). It is then that Moses builds an altar and says: "Because a hand is on the throne of the Lord, a war for the Lord against Amalek from generation to generation" (17:16).

Reading these final verses of the Amalek story in relation to the Psalms verses, the *midrash* asserts that the biblical description of a hand on the throne is looking toward a future time. God will one day eradicate Amalek's memory. Meanwhile, from generation to generation, God is at war with Amalek. And, during this time, God is not yet fully king. When God at some future time will eradicate the memory of Amalek—only then will God sit fully enthroned as Lord over the earth. At that time, God's throne will be established in justice and righteousness (Psalm 9:5, 8-9).

What it means, then, for Amalek to be the enemy of God is that the existence of Amalek is a limitation on God's dominion. God cannot fully be Lord while Amalek exists.

THE PRIMORDIAL FOE

These two understandings of Amalek—the internal and the external—mirror two contrasting perspectives on the presence of evil in the world. As has been articulated frequently in discussions of theodicy, it is impossible to postulate a perfectly good God who is infinitely powerful and to account for a world in which evil is real. Either evil is an illusion, or God is not perfectly good, or God is not infinitely powerful. To take evil seriously as a real element of the world and of our experience of the world means either to assume that God is not perfectly good or that God is not infinitely powerful.

If we assume that God is perfectly good and also that there is evil in the world, we have two main options. One option is to posit a perfectly created world perfectly ruled by God—in which case evil must be seen as some kind of falling away from that perfection. (Though, of course, we are left with the conundrum of how something in God's perfect creation could have fallen away from that perfection and become the source of evil in the world.) The other option is to posit that God is perfectly good but that God is *not* (at least as God manifests in our world) infinitely powerful—that, in some way, God does not perfectly rule over the world. According to this latter perspective, in other words, the existence of evil attests to God's incomplete dominion in the world as we know it.

These two perspectives on evil are contradictory but at the same time can be seen to complement each other. The first of these views is the one that is more familiar within mainstream Jewish tradition, and it is the one that is given priority in the creation story with which the Torah begins. The first chapter of Genesis describes a process of the unfolding of goodness. Each day God adds to the process of creation, layering good creation upon good creation like a succession of transparencies in an old anatomy textbook. At no point is anything missing, at no point is there a sense of struggle. Each day simply brings something new until God judges at the end of the sixth day that the created world is "very good" (Genesis 1:31).

The second perspective is familiar from the creation stories of neighboring ancient Near Eastern cultures. These stories are characterized by a cosmic battle between the chief god and other gods or goddesses, in particular gods or monsters of the sea, who threaten to drown the world in chaos. The chief god achieves victory in battle, is declared king, and is enthroned in a palace from which he exercises dominion over the earth.

In fact, Umberto Cassuto argues that this myth was well-known in the biblical world and that the creation story in Genesis goes out of its way to negate the idea that God's creation of the world involved a struggle with other deities. According to Cassuto, for example, *tehom*—"the deep" mentioned at the beginning of the creation story (1:2)—recalls Tiamat, the goddess of the chaotic waters against whom the creator god does battle in some of the cosmic myths. But the *tehom* of Genesis is not engaged in battle; it is an undeified substance, a backdrop to God's uncontested and irenic act of creation.

Similarly, Cassuto points out the unusual mention of the *tanninim* in the fifth day's account of the creation of sea creatures (1:21): it is the only time that a specific creature is mentioned, and its creation is described with the marked word *va-yivra*, a verb otherwise reserved in Genesis 1 for the introduction of the entire creation (1:1) and for the creation of the human being (1:27). The *tanninim*, Cassuto argues, recall the sea monsters with which it could be thought that God had to do battle in order to create the world. By listing them specifically as something that God simply created, along with all of God's other creations, the Torah is emphasizing that they have no special status and that there is no cosmic struggle underlying the world that we inhabit.

So the account of creation with which the Torah begins is not only entirely opposite to the common conception in the ancient Near East; according to Cassuto it takes that conception into account and strives to undermine it. There is no struggle; there are no competing forces. There is only a single God who creates a good world.

But Cassuto, like many other scholars, also notes that other biblical texts, and in particular poetic texts, make frequent mention of a battle between God and the chaotic forces of the sea. Psalm 74, for example, describes God's wondrous creation of the world, preceding mention of day and night, sun and moon (v. 16) with an account of God's destruction of the sea monsters:

> [13]You divided the sea with your might,
> you broke the heads of the *tanninim* in the waters.
> [14]You shattered the heads of Leviathan....

It is unclear how the authors and audiences of these texts understood these references. Did they understand them to refer to actual battles between God and other divine or semi-divine forces? Or were the images of a cosmic battle simply a metaphor within Israelite culture for the ways in which God imposes God's will over the world? Cassuto believes that the latter is the case. In his opinion, ancient myths of cosmic battle have been transformed in Israelite culture into a symbol of ethical and national import. The demonic forces against whom God does battle represent evildoers, those who refuse to obey God's will. The victory of God over these forces represents the imposition of God's will, the establishment of a just order, and often the deliverance of God's people.

I will leave open the question of whether the biblical texts that tell of a cosmic battle between God and the sea understood this battle literally or metaphorically. I want, rather, to focus on the meaning of this battle within the biblical texts that explicitly incorporate them, and then I want to show that elements of God's battle against the sea are echoed in the narrative of the Torah as well.

As Cassuto notes, God's battle against the sea in biblical texts goes beyond the idea that God is Lord, that God is ascendant over other divine or semi-divine figures, and that God is king. In biblical texts, God's kingship, established through God's victory in battle against the sea, means God's dominion over the world as a *just* ruler. Poetic texts that refer to this battle often include references to concepts such as *tzedek* and *mishpat* (righteousness and justice). For example, Psalm 89 describes God's creation of and dominion over the world in relation to God's vanquishing and taming of the sea, here embodied in the sea-monster Rahab:

> [10]You rule the raging of the sea;
> when its waves surge, you still them.
> [11]You crushed Rahab like a corpse;
> with your mighty arm you scattered your enemies. ...
>
> [15]Righteousness and justice are the foundation of your throne;
> ḥesed and truth go before you.

What it means for God to be king, to be ascendant over opposing forces, is that the forces of evil do not have sway, and the world is infused with justice.

Further, in some biblical passages, God's victory against the sea is portrayed as a way in which God redeemed God's people. Here, justice takes a *national* form, in that evildoers, those who challenge God's kingship, have subjugated God's people. To redeem that people means both to assert God's kingship and to subdue the evildoers who would abuse the innocent. God's battle against the sea, then, is seen to have occurred in primordial times, but it is also seen as the paradigm of a *recurring* battle. Isaiah 51 offers a particularly striking example of the use of this paradigm:

> [7]Listen to me, those who know righteousness,
> a people in whose heart is my teaching. ...
> [8]... my righteousness will be forever,
> and my salvation for all generations.
> [9]Awake, awake, put on might,
> O arm of the Lord!
> Awake as in days of old,
> generations of long ago!
> Was it not you who hacked Rahab in pieces,
> who pierced the *tannin*?
> [10]Was it not you who dried up the sea,
> the waters of the great deep (*tehom*),
> who made the depths of the sea
> a way for the redeemed to cross over?
> [11]So the ransomed of the Lord shall return,
> and come to Zion with singing....

This passage juxtaposes God's creation of the world with God's anticipated redemption of God's people. God's people are those who know justice (51:7), and God's justice and salvation are for all generations (51:8). Those divine attributes are expressed in God's vanquishing of evil. Verses 9 and 10 offer a striking conflation of God's primordial battle against the chaotic forces of the sea and of the parting of the sea in the Exodus story. God is said to have destroyed the sea monsters (Rahab and the *tannin*) and to have dried up the waters of the deep. Read sequentially, the drying up of the sea would seem to refer to the act of creation: God does battle against the sea, slaying the monsters and subduing the forces of chaos, pushing aside the watery deep and making room for the created world. But, continuing on, the drying of the sea takes on a different meaning:

God pushed aside the waters of the sea at the time of the Exodus from Egypt, to make room for God's people to cross over from enslavement to freedom. The first part of verse 10, then, is multivalent—the drying up of the sea is *both* the act of God at creation and the act of God at liberation. Established as a paradigmatic act, rather than a one-time past event, God's vanquishing of the sea offers a paradigm for anticipated redemption from the forces of evil as well.

In sum, these and many similar poetic biblical texts retain the memory of a battle between God and the sea. This battle represents God's fight against the forces of chaos and evil, and God's victory over the sea figures God's vanquishing of those forces and culminates in God's just dominion over the world. The primordial battle against the sea, though, turns out to be paradigmatic—it took place at creation, it took place at the Exodus, and it is anticipated in the future, when God once again will come to redeem God's people from those who oppress them.

But the very paradigmatic nature of this battle, holding out as it does the hope of redemption by means of God's mighty arm stretched out to destroy the foe, implies also that the foe still exists. God's battle against the sea, in other words, is not a battle that was won once and for all. It is an ongoing or recurring battle. The sea *always* threatens to overwhelm the world in chaos and destruction.

THE SONG OF THE SEA

In Isaiah 51, as noted, the splitting of the sea at the Exodus is conflated with the primordial battle against the sea. I want to suggest that this is not just a conceit of the prophetic text. Rather, within the Exodus narrative itself, God's deliverance of God's people is described in terms that relate to a cosmic battle. This is expressed in particular in the Song of the Sea, which employs words and phrases that are common to biblical poetic texts about God's vanquishing of the sea. The twist here, as Cassuto notes, is that God's power over the sea is deployed to destroy God's enemies. That is, it is not the sea *per se* that is God's enemy; God *has* control over the sea. Rather, it is those who threaten God's people who are God's enemies. They are destroyed by means of God's control of the waters of the sea, described in language used elsewhere to tell of God's victory over the sea itself.

But it is not only the Song's language and imagery that reflect the tradition of God's battle with the sea. The trajectory of the Song closely parallels the sequence of events in ancient Near Eastern texts that tell about the victory of the god in his battle with the sea. For example, in the Enuma Elish, the Babylonian creation epic, Marduk establishes his kingship by doing battle against Tiamat. Marduk deploys the winds to split Tiamat apart. He divides her in two, setting half of her up to form the sky, and posting guards to keep her waters from escaping. He goes on to create the luminaries through which the seasons are ordered and to establish dry land over the lower waters. And finally, he builds a palace from which he rules over the world, and the other gods proclaim his kingship.

The similarities between this narrative and the creation story in Genesis 1 are striking and have been pointed out by many scholars. As Cassuto and others have noted, though, and as has been mentioned above, the creation story denies the superhuman nature of the chaotic waters—the *tehom* of Genesis 1:2—and omits any suggestion of a conflict between God and any other forces. God's wind simply hovers over the waters (1:2), and God separates the waters into upper and lower waters and gathers the lower waters into oceans, making room for dry land, by means of God's word (1:6-10). There is no battle, no slaying of another god, no building of the world from the body of a slain deity.

The Exodus story, though, is different. Here, God *is* engaged in a contest with other gods. The stated purpose of the plagues is not just to force the Egyptians to free the Israelites. God wants to demonstrate God's dominion. "For this time I am sending all of my plagues upon your heart and upon your servants and upon your people," God says, introducing the seventh plague, the plague of hail, "in order that you will know that there is none like me in all the earth" (Exodus 9:14). "And I will pass through the land of Egypt on this night, and I will strike every firstborn in the land of Egypt… and against all the gods of Egypt I will execute judgments; I am Y-H-V-H" (12:12). The biblical text is not denying the existence of other gods; it is declaring that there is no god like Y-H-V-H. And that is what is affirmed in the Song of the Sea: "Who is like you among the gods, Y-H-V-H?!" (15:11).

In the Song, the Israelites, who earlier had not known God and had been ignorant as to God's identity (3:13-15), now identify God as Y-H-V-H and as a man of war (15:3). They celebrate God's destruction of the Egyptians by means of the waters of *tehom* (15:5) and God's demonstration of power over the waters of *tehom*, which God pushed aside by a blast of wind (15:8; compare the description of the splitting of the sea and the emergence of dry land in 14:21) and, again with a blast of wind, blew back over the Egyptians (15:10). It is then, after describing God's conquest of God's enemies by means of God's control over the sea, that the Israelites declare "Who is like you among the gods, Y-H-V-H?! Who is like you, glorious in holiness, fearful in praises, doing wonders?!" (15:11). It is this God who leads God's people to redemption, guiding them in God's might to God's holy habitation (15:13). The Song ends with a reference to God's palace— the place that is established for God to dwell in, God's sanctuary (15:17). In other words, God's vanquishing of God's enemies and God's deliverance of God's people lead to God's enthronement. And so the Song culminates with a declaration of God's kingship: "The Lord (Y-H-V-H) will reign for ever and ever" (15:18).

The Song of the Sea, then, offers an alternative, agonistic creation story. Here, God does battle against God's enemies—the unjust Egyptians and their gods. God asserts control over the sea, reenacting the primordial act of conquest in order to vanquish God's enemies. The battle, God's act of war, demonstrates God's ascendancy as Lord over other gods. God is declared king, and the Song looks toward a time when God will take the throne in the sanctuary/palace toward which God is leading God's people.

A *midrash* on the introductory words to the Song of the Sea picks up on this meaning of the Israelites' song:

> "Then (*az*) sang Moses" (Exodus 15:1)—
> This is as is written:
> "Your throne is established from old (*az*)" (Psalm 93:2).
> Rabbi Berekhiah said in the name of Rabbi Abahu:
> Even though you are from eternity,
> your throne was not established
> and you were not made known in your world
> until your children spoke a song.
> Thus it says: "Your throne is established from *az*."
> It is analogous to a king who waged war and was victorious
> and they made him into an emperor.
> They said to him: Until you waged war you were a king,
> now we have made you an emperor....
> From when you stood at the sea

and we spoke a song before you with *az*,
your kingship was set and your throne was established.
Thus—"Your throne was established from *az*"—
at *az yashir* ("Then sang").

Shemot Rabbah 23:1

The *midrash* juxtaposes the word *az*—"then"—in the introduction to the Song of the Sea with the word *az* in Psalm 93. Psalm 93 is a brief psalm that celebrates God's kingship. Making reference to God's vanquishing of the sea, the psalm speaks of the establishment of God's dominion over the earth: "Your throne is established from old (*az*)." The psalm, of course, is referring to God's struggle with the sea in primordial times. But the *midrash* makes a striking claim. God's throne, says the *midrash*, was *not* established at the beginning of time. Rather, God's throne was established from *az*, from "then." And what "then" is the psalm referring to? The "then" at which Moses and the Israelites sang their song—*az yashir*. The *midrash* is seeing the victory against the Egyptians that the Song celebrates as a culmination of the primordial battle with the sea. At creation, God became king; but only at the Exodus does God become emperor. God's consummate dominion is only established when God vanquishes the Egyptian enemy and splits the sea for the redeemed people to pass through. It is then that God's dominion is declared by God's people, and God reigns supreme.

In fact, the book of Exodus as a whole can be seen as an alternative creation story. It begins with language that recalls the beginning of Genesis: for example, the children of Israel increase and multiply (Exodus 1:7); Moses's mother sees that he is good (2:2); she saves the baby by placing him in an ark (2:3). And it ends with the construction of God's sanctuary, described in words and phrases that again recall the creation of the world. But this is not a creation story that describes the unfolding of goodness that Genesis 1 portrays. The book of Exodus, instead, begins by describing a miserable world, a world in which the forces of evil and injustice are ascendant. It is a world in which God has to do battle. God has to fight against the forces of evil, to vanquish God's foes in order to lead the oppressed to redemption. God is forced to do battle in order to achieve dominion. And God's dominion, just as we noted in many of the poetic texts that describe God's primordial vanquishing of the foe, is a dominion of justice. And so, when the book of Exodus ends with the building of God's sanctuary, the seat of God's kingship, it anticipates the ultimate holy abode that is described in the Song, the ascendancy to the throne that follows God's vanquishing of the enemy.

God's battle against the Egyptians as a type of the primordial battle against the sea is alluded to in Ezekiel's prophecy against his contemporary Pharaoh, who is imagined as a great sea-monster (*tannim*, an alternative spelling of *tannin*):

> ³Speak and say: Thus said the Lord God:
> Behold, I am against you Pharaoh, king of Egypt,
> the great *tannim* who crouches within its rivers,
> who said "My Nile is mine, and I made it for myself."
> ⁴I will put hooks in your jaws,
> and I will make the fish of your rivers cling to your scales,
> and I will haul you up from within your rivers....
> ⁵And I will abandon you to the wilderness...
> to the beasts of the earth and to the birds of the sky
> I have given you as food.
> ⁶And all of the inhabitants of Egypt
> shall know that I am the Lord....
>
> *Ezekiel 29:3-6*

This passage from Ezekiel was chosen as the *haftarah* for Va'Era, the Torah portion in which Moses and Aaron begin to do wonders in the presence of Pharaoh. The first of these wonders is the transformation of Aaron's rod into a *tannin* (Exodus 7:10)—and it is noteworthy that, here, the rod turns into a *tannin*, not a snake as Moses's rod had become during his initial encounter with God at the burning bush (4:3). The biblical narrative's evocation of the *tannin* here thrusts into our consciousness the primordial narrative, signaling that God's battle against Pharaoh and the Egyptians is a battle of cosmic proportions—it is nothing other than God's battle against the forces of evil, and the anticipated vanquishing of the Egyptians is nothing other than God's ascendancy as Lord of the world to the throne of justice. That is what Ezekiel is reflecting as well. Pharaoh—in this case, the Pharaoh of Ezekiel's time—casts himself as a god: it is he who made the Nile, and he is the lord of the rivers in which he dwells. But God will fish him out of the Nile, asserting his own dominion over this would-be god, and will throw the *tannim*-Pharaoh into the desert, to be devoured by wild beasts and birds.

Similar imagery appears in Ezekiel 32, the dirge that Ezekiel is commanded to raise for Pharaoh. Here, too, Pharaoh is a *tannim* whom God fishes out of the waters. The *tannim*'s flesh is thrust on the hills, and his blood flows down the hills into the watercourses. Finally, at the death of the *tannim*, God darkens the stars and covers the sun with a cloud, plunging Pharaoh's land into darkness (Ezekiel 32:2-8). Ezekiel is recalling the first and penultimate plagues that God brought against the Egyptians in the book of Exodus: blood and darkness. The plague of blood, here, is understood as the filling of the waters with the blood of the slain god—Pharaoh, who is the *tannim*. And the luminaries' light is taken away from the Egyptians through the death of their god, thus countering God's first act of creation and plunging the land of Egypt into the chaotic and terrifying state of a world that God has destroyed. It is noteworthy that the conquest of the foe is juxtaposed with the luminaries as well in Enuma Elish, in which Marduk forms the luminaries after vanquishing Tiamat. And a similar juxtaposition appears in Psalm 136 (*hodu*), which moves abruptly from the creation of the luminaries to the destruction of the Egyptians. While death of the enemy god, then, spells darkness and destruction for the foe, it heralds the creation of a new or renewed world in which the victorious god reigns supreme.

The plagues, on this reading, are not just wonders that God instructs Moses and Aaron to do in order to prove God's power to Pharaoh and the Egyptians. The plagues—in particular, the plagues of blood and darkness—are manifestations of a mighty battle between God and God's enemy, the would-be god against whom God needs to do battle and whom God must vanquish in order to achieve dominion over the world.

It is this victory that the Song of the Sea celebrates. In a deployment of God's power over the sea, God has destroyed the Egyptian foe, the people who were pursuing God's own people (Exodus 15:4-12). And God is leading God's people to redemption, bringing them toward God's holy abode (15:13). The nations, continues the Song, hear this and are terrified; the Philistines, the Edomites, the Moabites, the Canaanites—all are gripped by fear and trembling (15:14-15). And the Israelites, God's people, cross over, undeterred by anyone (15:16). They come to God's dwelling place, to the sanctuary from which God will reign as king forever (15:17). And they declare God's kingship (15:18).

But "Amalek came" (17:8). The battle waged by Amalek is narrated just two chapters after the crossing of the sea. Amalek is the one nation that is not afraid; Amalek comes to wage war on God's people. In the words of Deuteronomy, Amalek *does not fear God*. Amalek will not step aside to allow God to lead God's people to the holy place; Amalek will not allow God's sanctuary to be built; Amalek will not allow God to reign as king. Amalek "came"—apparently, Amalek was not situated in Israel's path. Rather, Amalek comes from far away to stop the trajectory of redemption and the establishment of God's dominion. Amalek comes to do battle with God.

ESTABLISHING GOD'S DOMINION

Amalek, according to this perspective, is the residue of God's primordial foe. God's victory is not complete; God's kingship is not uncontested. This is what the *midrash* with which we began is pointing out. God's throne is not complete and God's name is not complete, and they cannot be complete until the name of Amalek will be completely obliterated. Only once God's foe is destroyed will God fully reign as king over the world. Only once the enemy is destroyed will the words of the Psalmist come true: "But the Lord (Y-H-V-H) will sit forever; he has established his throne (*kis'o*) in justice" (Psalm 9:8).

This reading is reflected in the verses that are appended to the Song of the Sea in liturgical practice. After the declaration of God's kingship— "The Lord will reign forever and ever!" (Exodus 15:18)—and the following verse, three additional verses are recited:

> "For kingship is the Lord's,
> and he rules over the nations" (Psalm 22:29).

> "And redeemers shall rise up on Mount Zion
> to wreak judgment on Mount Esau,
> and kingship will be the Lord's" (Obadiah 1:21).

> "And the Lord will be king over all the earth;
> on that day the Lord will be one and his name one"
> (Zechariah 14:9).

Each of these three verses expands upon the theme of God's kingship that is proclaimed at the end of the Song. The first verse asserts that God is king over all of the nations. But the second verse thrusts this vision into the future: "kingship *will be* the Lord's." Only once God wreaks judgment on Mount Esau will God fully be king. The third verse plays out this future vision: "*on that day* the Lord will be one and his name one"—in the future, after God vanquishes God's enemy, "the Lord will be king over all the earth."

In this liturgical addendum to the Song, the enemy that God has yet to vanquish is Esau/Edom, understood as the archenemy of Israel. It is Edom, too, that is the enemy in the *midrash* that Rashi cites about God's eternal war with Amalek. In order to demonstrate that the enemy that God will reduce to eternal ruin in Psalm 9:7 is Edom, Rashi quotes Amos's prophecy against Edom: "and he kept his wrath forever" (Amos 1:11). Edom is Esau (Genesis 36:1), and Esau is the grandfather of Amalek (36:12).

In fact, in the book of Numbers, Edom tries to block the Israelites on their way to the promised land. The brief story in which Moses asks the king of Edom to allow the Israelites to cross through his territory includes the verb "to cross over" seven times (Numbers 20:17-21). The Song of the Sea speaks of the Israelites "crossing over" into God's land in which God's sanctuary will be established, while all of the nations, Edom included, are gripped by fear (Exodus 15:14-17). Amalek though, as we saw, comes shortly after, threatening to block the Israelites as they continue on their journey. Now, forty years later, Edom refuses to allow the Israelites to cross over into their destined land, threatening them with war should they try to advance. Notably, the story is introduced with the words: "And Moses sent messengers" (Numbers 20:14), recalling the story in which Jacob was on his way back to the land of Canaan after years of exile and sends messengers to his brother Esau (Genesis 32:4). And so Jacob's return to Canaan, the Israelites' crossing the sea after leaving Egypt, and the Israelites' crossing over into the promised land all involve an encounter with Esau or his descendants. Edom/Esau/Amalek is the nation who always stands between Israel and the promised land, who always threatens the establishment of God's dwelling place.

And so, in liturgical practice, recitation of the Song of the Sea culminates with the anticipation that God will wreak judgment on Esau/Amalek. Once God brings this eternal enemy to ruin, kingship will be the Lord's.

Then—"on that day"—God will establish God's throne in justice and will reign over all the earth.

These verses transform the meaning of our practice of reciting the Song during morning prayers. Reciting the Song of the Sea at the very end of Pesukei de-Zimra, the section of the liturgy that focuses on praise of God and that sets the stage for the core section of the statutory liturgy, is an expression of gratitude to God as redeemer, a proclamation of God's kingship, and a positioning of the pray-er or the praying community as the people who, redeemed by God, are those whose task it is to declare God as king. Adding the concluding verses shifts this picture dramatically. God *is* the redeemer; we, the redeemed, *do* recognize God's kingship—but there are others who *do not* recognize God as king. There is an enemy who continues to do battle with God and with God's people and, as long as that enemy exists, the proclamation of God's kingship must be understood as anticipatory. *We* recognize God as king, but God is not yet fully king. Only "on that day" will the Lord "be king over all the earth."

The world in which we live, then, is a dynamic universe that is caught in a battle between God and the enemy, between good and evil, between justice and injustice. Standing in prayer and in praise of God, we find ourselves caught up in this battle. We throw our weight on the side of God's kingship, but we recognize that the battle is not over and that a vision of God's dominion over the world is a vision of a future time, not a picture of the world as it is.

FIGHTING INJUSTICE

Whose task *is* it to fight Amalek? In Exodus, it is God's task. "Write this as a memorial in a book and put it in the ears of Joshua, that *I* will utterly blot out the memory/name of Amalek from under the heavens" (Exodus 17:14). But in Deuteronomy, the eradication of Amalek's name is formulated as a command: "And it shall be, when the Lord your God gives you rest from all your enemies around you, in the land that the Lord your God is giving you as an inheritance to possess it, *you* shall blot out the memory/name of Amalek from under the heavens—do not forget!" (Deuteronomy 25:19). The battle against Amalek is God's battle: "a war for the Lord against Amalek from generation to generation" (Exodus 17:16). But God's people are called to fight that battle. In our daily morning prayers, the moment before we begin the blessings that introduce the Shema, the declaration of God's kingship, we remind ourselves that the battle for God's dominion in the world is still in progress and that *we* have a role to play in this dynamic process.

The human element of this process is captured in the Talmud's discussion of the three things that the Israelites are to do when they come to the promised land: appoint a king, destroy Amalek, and build the Temple (Bavli Sanhedrin 20b). The Talmud asserts that these things have to take place in a particular order. Working with verses from Deuteronomy and Samuel, the Talmud shows that Amalek must be destroyed before the Temple can be built. The verse from Samuel is particularly salient: King David seeks to build God's house after "the Lord had given him rest from all his enemies around him" (2 Samuel 7:1, echoing Deuteronomy 25:19, the injunction to destroy Amalek). It is not possible to build God's sanctuary while Amalek is present in the world. The Song of the Sea made that clear: when all of the nations step aside and allow God to be king, then God's dwelling place on earth can exist. If Amalek comes and challenges God's kingship, then God's palace/sanctuary cannot yet be built. So Amalek will have to be destroyed before the Temple is built.

What about appointing a king? The king, the Talmud tells us, must be appointed first, because it is the king's job to destroy Amalek. This is clear from the book of Samuel. Saul's downfall is his failure to destroy Amalek (1 Samuel 15). The Talmud derives that appointing a king must precede the destruction of Amalek from the verse in Exodus that talks about God's war with Amalek: "Because a hand is on the throne of the Lord, a war for the Lord against Amalek…" (Exodus 17:16). The Talmud understands the throne in this verse to refer to human kingship. What it means to be a king of Israel is that a human being is occupying the terrestrial counterpart of God's celestial throne. If God is at war with Amalek, then the king must fight God's battle. To fail to eradicate Amalek means that you are not king—you have failed to do the task of the king.

This mirroring of human and divine kingship is portrayed vividly in Psalm 89, quoted earlier to demonstrate the association of God's cosmic battle with God's dominion of justice:

> [4]"I have made a covenant with my chosen one,
> I have sworn to my servant David:

⁵"'I will establish your descendants forever,
and build your throne for all generations.'" ...

⁹O Lord, God of hosts,
who is as mighty as you, O Lord?
Your faithfulness surrounds you.
¹⁰You rule the raging of the sea;
when its waves surge, you still them.
¹¹You crushed Rahab like a corpse;
with your mighty arm you scattered your enemies.
¹²The heavens are yours, the earth also is yours;
the world and all that is in it—you have established them. ...

¹⁴You have a mighty arm;
strong is your hand, high your right hand.
¹⁵Righteousness and justice are the foundation of your throne;
hesed and truth go before you. ...

²⁰Then you spoke in a vision to your pious ones, and said:
"I have set the crown on one who is mighty,
I have exalted one chosen from the people.
²¹I have found my servant David;
with my holy oil I have anointed him;
²²my hand shall always remain with him;
my arm also shall strengthen him.
²³The enemy shall not outwit him,
the wicked shall not humble him.
²⁴I will crush his foes before him
and strike down those who hate him. ...

²⁶I will set his hand on the sea
and his right hand on the rivers."

In these verses, as throughout the psalm, God's kingship is juxtaposed with David's kingship. God's lordship over heaven and earth is instantiated by God's vanquishing of the sea (89:9-11), and God will set the terrestrial king's hand over sea and rivers (89:26). God, whose own throne is founded on righteousness and justice (89:15), establishes David's eternal throne (89:5). And so, by implication, David's own throne has to be a throne of justice. David has to fight evil, and David has to establish justice.

This is what David, unlike Saul, accomplishes in the book of Samuel. Amalek has destroyed a town called Ziklag and taken the women and children into captivity (1 Samuel 30:1-3). David vanquishes Amalek and rescues all of the captives (30:17-19). But then some of David's men insist on taking for themselves all of the property that has been recovered and not returning any of it to the men who had been too exhausted to join the battle (30:22). David refuses to go along with this, asserting that everyone should take his share of the property (30:23-24). And this becomes a *ḥok u-mishpat*—a statute and judgment—for all time (30:25). So David not only vanquishes Amalek, the enemy who yet again, as at the time of the Exodus, preys on the weak. David establishes just rules, protecting those who are weak from the greed of the powerful. It is at this moment that David's kingship is assured. Saul is killed in battle in the very next chapter, making way for David to assume the throne. And, when David's kingship over all of Israel is cemented, it is a kingship characterized by the doing of justice: "And David reigned over all of Israel, and David did *mishpat u-tzdakah*—judgment and justice—for all of his people" (2 Samuel 8:15).

In Exodus, too, the vanquishing of Amalek is juxtaposed with the instituting of justice. Right after the Amalek episode, Jethro comes to visit Moses. He rejoices about God's redemption of the Israelites from Egyptian domination and about God's salvation of the people from their troubles along the way (Exodus 18:8-9). "Now I know," he says, "that the Lord is greater than all gods" (18:11). God's greatness is not only God's demonstration of power against Israel's—and God's—enemies; it is God's doing of justice, God's deliverance of the weak from the hand of those who attempt to take advantage of them. The next day, Jethro sees the people standing from morning till evening, waiting for Moses to judge their cases. Jethro advises Moses how to build a system in which the people will have access to judges, and in which Moses will be able to teach them God's laws and the ways in which they should conduct themselves. If Amalek refuses to acknowledge the God who seeks to establish a dominion of justice, then the vanquishing of Amalek makes space for a world in which a just society can be built, a world in which God has dominion. And, of course, the people's seeking of judgment and Moses's establishment of a system of justice herald the giving of the Torah and the setting out of God's *mishpatim*—judgments—in the chapters immediately following.

The scribal practice of blotting out the word "Amalek" before setting out to write a Torah scroll captures this dynamic. "Write this as a memorial in a book," God tells Moses after Amalek has been defeated, "that I will utterly blot out the memory/name of Amalek from under the heavens" (17:14). It is noteworthy that the first thing that the Torah commands to write is not Torah; it is the remembrance to obliterate the memory of Amalek. We can only write the Torah after we have crossed out the name of Amalek, because Torah begins where Amalek ends. And, of course, with the receiving of the Torah comes the command to build the tabernacle. Paralleling the rabbinic understanding of the order of the things that the Israelites must do when they enter the promised land, and paralleling the trajectory of the Song of the Sea, in the narrative of the book of Exodus, God's palace, God's dwelling place on earth, can only be built after the destruction of the forces of injustice that strive to limit God's dominion.

The book of Exodus traces a trajectory toward God's dominion on earth, toward justice, toward knowledge of God. The story of Amalek reminds us that that trajectory is interrupted. The world is not fully just, God is not fully known and, in rabbinic imagination, the Temple is destroyed by Edom, Amalek's forebearer. Amalek is *always* working to keep God from ruling the world with justice. And we are eternally called to engage in the war against Amalek.

This war is not fought only on the battlefield. Recalling the juxtaposition in Exodus between the battle against Amalek and the seeking of justice, it is noteworthy that, in Deuteronomy, the commandment to remember Amalek and to eradicate its memory is positioned at the very end of the long series of laws that Moses teaches the people. The final law before the Amalek passage is the law against false measures. "You shall have a perfect and just weight; you shall have a perfect and just measure… because all who do these things are an abomination to the Lord your God, all who do unrighteousness" (Deuteronomy 25:15-16). Justice here takes the most private form—it relates to what is in your home and what is in your pocket (25:13-14). It is the doing of justice, the rejection of unrighteousness, allowing the call of justice to permeate even the recesses of our behavior and our selves, that pushes back Amalek and its always-threatening desire to challenge the dominion of the God of justice in the world. The ways in which we behave, on the largest and the smallest scales, can extend the compass of God's dominion in the face of that which always threatens it.

GOODNESS AND EVIL

The Torah begins with the creation of light, the separation of the waters, and the gathering of the waters into the seas, making room for the land on which God will plant vegetation and put animals and human beings. It is a story of the unfolding of goodness and order, a story that offers a vision of a perfect world ruled by a God who is good and all-powerful. The possibility of evil or of something that is not good enters the biblical story only after the creation of the human being (Genesis 2:9, 18; note the absence in Genesis 1 of "and God saw that it was good" after the creation of the human being). Adam's disobedience to God's command plunges humankind into a succession of sinful behavior, beginning with Adam's son, Cain, and continuing throughout the biblical story. This irenic view of creation by an all-powerful good creator correlates with an understanding of evil as related to human failure.

But the Torah hints at an alternative vision of the world as having emerged from an agonistic creation. This is a world in which evil has sway and in which God is pitted in an eternal battle against the forces of evil and chaos and injustice. Amalek is the form that the residue of these forces takes in our national story. Until some future time when Amalek will be destroyed, it cannot be said that the world is a place in which God has complete dominion. Meanwhile, human beings have a role to play, because they are bidden to join God's battle against this foe.

These two visions represent conflicting perspectives on the place of evil in the world. The presence of both of these perspectives within Jewish religious imagination offers different options that might resonate with different experiences, different historical moments, or different times in our lives. And the different understandings of Amalek—and of whose lack of fear of God allows Amalek to come—offer different challenges within religious life.

The internal view of Amalek asks me to look inside myself. What is it within me that is blocking me from crossing over to the promised land? What in me is not matching up to that picture that God showed the sea when God created the world? What is it in me or in us that does not fear God, that hesitates to acknowledge God's presence in our midst, that keeps us from building God's sanctuary? God created a good world; what about us and our choices is keeping God's plan from working out?

The alternative view starts from a different place. I look at the world, and it's not a good place. And I can't believe that the evil in the world is because of choices I've made or my community has made. The external view of Amalek allows me to say that maybe it's not yet a good world. Maybe God doesn't yet have full dominion; maybe creation is still in process. One day God's name will be complete, but not yet. One day God will reign supreme, but not yet. I am not responsible for the evil that is in the world. But I am responsible to ask myself what I can do to make more room for good, to push back the dominion of evil, to expand God's dominion.

THE ROARING OF THE SEA

On the third day [of creation]...
the waters were covering the entire surface of the earth.
And when speech went forth from the mighty one,
"Let the waters be gathered" (Genesis 1:9)
...the waters rolled down and were gathered into the valleys....
At once the waters exalted themselves
and rose to cover the earth as at the beginning,
until the Blessed Holy One scolded them and conquered them
and put them under the soles of his feet...
and made the sand a boundary for the ocean....
And when they rise and see the sand before them,
they return backward,
as it says:
"'Will you not fear me?' says the Lord.
'Will you not tremble at my presence,
who placed the sand as a boundary for the sea,
[a perpetual decree that it cannot pass it?
They toss but cannot prevail,
and the waves roar but cannot pass it]' (Jeremiah 5:22)."

Pirkei de-Rabbi Eliezer 5

The Jeremiah verse with which this *midrash* concludes offers an image of powerful waves moving closer and closer to land but then crashing onto the shore and pulling back. In Jeremiah's imagination, the sea, subordinated to God's will at creation, is always pushing up against God's dominion, always threatening to undo God's creation and restore the world to chaos. But God has placed a boundary for the sea, and so the sea is always forced to retreat.

The *midrash* expands on this, imagining the very act of creation as a contest between God and the sea. The sea resists God's power, but God tramples the sea, setting a boundary for it that it cannot pass. The *midrash* calls to mind the agonistic view of creation hinted at in biblical texts, the sea representing powerful forces that challenge God and against which God needs to do battle.

And yet, while the sea is subdued by God, it does not give up. The Jeremiah verse and its midrashic elaboration summon an image with which we are all familiar, an experience of watching the sea crashing up against the shore and retreating, only to gather force and come near again with the next wave. This familiar image of a natural occurrence becomes transmuted into a dynamic scene of an eternal foe subdued but not yet fully vanquished, an eternal enemy always straining to break its bounds and gain control.

Refracted by these texts, the scene calls to our imagination the entire arc of the biblical narrative on both a national and cosmic scale: the primordial watery chaos that gives way to God's act of orderly creation, the splitting of the sea to enable God's redeemed people to pass, and of course the eternal battle against Amalek. The image of ocean waves becomes a powerful reminder that the threatening enemy is always there. It might be held at bay, but it has not disappeared. The forces of chaos, injustice, and destruction challenge God's dominion from generation to generation.

THE HIDDEN AND THE REVEALED

The hidden things are for the Lord our God
but the revealed things are for us and our children forever
to do all of the words of this teaching.

Deuteronomy 29:28

There are dots above [the letters of] "for us and our children" and the *ayin* of "forever."
Why?

Thus said Ezra [the Scribe]:
"If Elijah comes and says: 'Why did you write thus?'
I will say: 'I put dots above them.'
And if he says: 'You wrote well,'
I will remove the dots from them."

Avot de-Rabbi Natan A 34

A VERSE THAT APPEARS toward the end of the book of Deuteronomy has dots above eleven of its letters. The verse itself is intriguing, besides this curious feature of its orthography, as it speaks of things both revealed and hidden. Within the rabbinic interpretive tradition, these two elements—the verse's orthography and its content—interact to generate a variety of understandings of the verse's meaning. These meanings speak to critical questions about responsibility and accountability, both individual and communal. For what actions are we responsible? Is a community held accountable for the actions of its individual members? In what ways might

I be responsible for my fellow's behavior? What are the limits, if any, of an individual's or community's responsibility for its own or others' actions?

We will begin our inquiry into the implications of this verse by looking at possible meanings of "the hidden things" and "the revealed things," paying special attention to the resonance of this verse within its biblical context. We will go on to look at rabbinic interpretations of the significance of the dots above eleven of the letters in the verse. We will then focus on the interpretation of the verse that seems best to fit its biblical context and that underlies the rabbinic interpretations of the significance of the dots—an interpretation that holds a community maximally responsible for the actions of its individual members—and we will examine a biblical story that instantiates this idea. We will consider possible understandings of the groundings of such a maximalist view of communal responsibility by examining the rabbinic concept of *areivut*. And we will look at metaphors of community offered by talmudic commentators and midrashic texts in order to imagine living in shared responsibility with other members of our community.

THE HIDDEN THINGS

The verse about the hidden and revealed things appears in one of Moses's final addresses to the Israelites, after Moses has concluded the long speech that constitutes most of the book of Deuteronomy, from chapter 5 through chapter 26. That speech, we are told at the very end of chapter 28, spells out the terms of a covenant that God has established with the people in the land of Moab, a covenant additional to the one established at Sinai (Deuteronomy 28:69). The following two chapters, chapters 29 and 30, are an exhortation to observe the covenant, including a warning against disobedience, an invitation to return to God should the people go astray, encouragement that the possibility of fulfilling the covenant is not out of reach, and a promise of the good that attends obeying the terms of the covenant. Our verse appears right in the middle of this exhortation, after Moses's dire warning about disobedience and its consequences.

But what *are* the hidden things and the revealed things? *Midrashim* and classical commentators offer three possible understandings, each of which focuses us on our accountability for our own or others' behavior.

The first raises the question of accountability for acts that we do not know are forbidden, the second addresses the challenge of atonement for wrong actions that we do not know we have done, and the third highlights the complex problem of a community's responsibility for the acts of its members.

The first possibility is that the hidden things are things that God has not revealed to the people, and the revealed things are things that God *has* revealed to the people. These things may be laws or other kinds of teachings or, perhaps, knowledge that might inform behavior. Such an understanding fits well with the conclusion of the verse: "but the revealed things are for us... to do all of the words of this teaching." According to this understanding, we are responsible to fulfill the revealed law, or to follow the revealed teachings, or to base our choices on what we are able to know, but we are *not* held accountable for laws or teachings or information that we cannot know. That the hidden things are laws that have not (yet) been revealed appears to be reflected in rabbinic *midrashim* such as Sifrei Bemidbar 69 ("You have done the revealed things; I will even make known to you the hidden things,") and Midrash Mishlei 26 ("You have not even been able to abide by what is revealed,") and it is reflected as well in Qumran texts that understand even the hidden things to have been revealed to the sect. This interpretation sees the verse as reassuring the people after the dire warning about the consequences of disobedience, in consonance with the passages that follow, which declare both repentance and the possibility of fulfilling God's word to be within reach (Deuteronomy 30:1-14). Although God holds you accountable and will punish you for your sins, the verse is saying, accountability is limited to that which you can know.

A second possibility is that "hidden things" refer to deeds that a person has done that are hidden from the person who has done them, while "revealed things" are deeds of which a person is aware. Ramban takes this to be the plain meaning of the Deuteronomy verse, citing the "hidden things" in Psalm 19:13: "Who can discern errors? Cleanse me from hidden things." Here, "hidden things" refers to sins both unintentional and unknown, as opposed to the intentional sins referred to in the following verse: "Also from willful sins keep your servant..." (Psalm 19:14). And so Ramban understands "the hidden things" in Deuteronomy to refer to "the sins which are hidden from the one who does them." These are acts for which we bear no responsibility—they are "for the Lord our God." "The revealed things," on the other hand, are the intentional sins, and for these we do bear responsibility. Since the covenant includes a curse against those who fail to fulfill God's commandments (Deuteronomy 27:26; 28:15), God is here reassuring the people that those who violate God's word unknowingly and unintentionally will not be included in the curse.

This understanding of the hidden things and the revealed things, in fact, provides the framing of the Yom Kippur Vidui (confession). The long list of sins that are recited first by the individual and then by the congregation is introduced by an assertion that God knows all hidden and revealed things and by a request for forgiveness of all sins:

> What can we say before you, who sits on high,
> and what can we relate before you, who dwells in the heavens?
> For all of the *hidden things* and *revealed things* you know. ...
>
> You know the mysteries of the world
> and the secret things that are *hidden* within all living beings. ...
> Nothing is secret from you,
> and nothing is *hidden* from before your eyes.
> And so, may it be your will, Lord our God and God of our ancestors,
> that you forgive us for all our sins
> and pardon us for all our iniquities
> and grant us atonement for all our transgressions.

The connection between God's knowledge of all things, hidden and revealed, and the request for forgiveness of all sins only becomes fully clear at the end of the confession. The long list of sins that we may have committed and for which we seek forgiveness concludes with "those that are *revealed* to us and those that are *not revealed* to us." The latter, it turns out, present a special problem, because the sins that we do *not* know about, the hidden things, are things that we cannot confess and for which we cannot properly repent. "Those that are *revealed* to us," we conclude, "we have already said them before you and confessed them to you. But those that are *not revealed* to us, before you they are *revealed* and known, as it is said: 'The hidden things are for the Lord our God, but the revealed things are for us and our children forever to do all of the words of this teaching.'"

The Hidden and the Revealed

In the context of the dire warning about disobedience to the terms of the covenant in the book of Deuteronomy, Ramban understood "the hidden things are for the Lord our God" as excusing people for inadvertent, unknowing acts. But in the context of Yom Kippur, the day on which we seek atonement, our liturgy understands the hidden things, those acts that we have done unwittingly and of which we are not aware, as both requiring atonement and as especially challenging to repent of. How can we regret, confess, and ask forgiveness for things that we do not even know that we did? For this especially we turn to God for help. "The revealed things" we confess; "the hidden things" are for God to forgive and grant atonement for, despite our inability to truly repent of those acts.

In fact, the liturgy goes on to quote the Psalms verse that Ramban cited to establish the meaning of "the hidden things": "Who can discern errors? Cleanse me from hidden things." The implication is clear: We are not held guiltless for the things that we have done that are hidden from us. We have no capacity to discern what we have done unintentionally and unknowingly, and yet we need to be cleansed of those very things. We turn to God, by whom both the hidden and the revealed things are known, to help us atone for the things that our own lack of knowledge and understanding make it impossible for us to confess and to repent of.

FROM INDIVIDUAL TO COMMUNITY

Both of these interpretations of "the hidden things" understand these things to be hidden from the individual who has sinned and understand the potential consequences of the person's act to devolve upon the person. A third interpretation differs in both respects, understanding the hidden things to be acts of an individual that are hidden *from the community* and the potential consequences of such acts as devolving upon the entire community.

The word "hidden" appears several times in the biblical passages that precede the enigmatic verse about the hidden and revealed things. Immediately after Moses concludes his extended teaching of the laws that the people are bound to obey and which constitute the terms of their covenant with God, Moses instructs the people that, when they cross the Jordan into the promised land, they are to set up stones on which they are to write the teaching, and he further instructs them to perform a ceremony of blessings and curses on Mount Gerizim and Mount Ebal (Deuteronomy 27). The Levites are to recite twelve curses, no doubt corresponding to the twelve tribes, six of whom stand on each of the mountains (27:12-13). Each of the curses anathematizes an individual who violates a specific commandment, with the final curse directed more generally against someone who does not fulfill the words of the Torah. Two of the curses specify acts that are done "in hiding": "cursed is the person who makes an idol… and places it in hiding" and "cursed is the person who strikes their fellow in hiding" (27:15, 24).

Why the emphasis on hidden crimes, and why is hiddenness specified only in relation to these two crimes? Rashbam, Ibn Ezra, Rav Yosef Kara, and others suggest that, in fact, each of the crimes whose committers are cursed are crimes that take place in private, crimes that others are unlikely to know about. For example, a man who sleeps with his father's wife is anathematized, as is a man who sleeps with his sister or with his mother-in-law (27:20, 22, 23), but a man who sleeps with a married woman is not. The former three sins are less likely to be noticed, because the man will not arouse suspicion by being in the same house as his stepmother or his sister or his mother-in-law, but he *would* be likely to arouse suspicion by entering his neighbor's house. Moving a boundary marker (27:17) and taking a bribe against an innocent person (27:25) are by their nature done secretly, and misdirecting a blind person (27:18) or corrupting the judgment of a helpless individual (27:19) are acts that will either be unnoticed or that have perpetrators that will not be identified or reported.

In contrast, the two acts that are said to be done "in hiding" are acts that, in general, are not necessarily done in private: a person might well set up an idol in sight of others, and a person could well strike their fellow in public. But the person who does either of these two things is not anathematized; the curses are directed only against someone who does one or the other of these acts *hiddenly*. The classical commentaries explain that there is no need to curse the person who does such an act openly; that person will be punished by the community. The curses are directed only at a person who does such an act hiddenly, because the community has no ability to punish such a person. And the same is true of the other acts that are listed in the series of curses, acts that are inherently private and likely to remain hidden from the community.

The Hidden and the Revealed

The special concern posed by acts that are done in hiding appears in a gruesome form in the chapter immediately following. The chapter spells out the blessings and curses that will befall the people should they follow God's commands or should they disobey them. The horrific curses are described at length and in excruciating detail, reaching their peak in a description of fathers who will be reduced to eating their own children and who will refuse to share them with their wives and remaining children and, finally, with a description of mothers who will eat their children—"in hiding" (28:53-57). As the curses are explicitly framed as a measure-for-measure response to the people's deeds (28:47-48), the notice that the mother's act will be done in hiding—whether because this allows her not to share with her family or because she is ashamed of this terrible act—echoing as it does the acts done in hiding in the preceding chapter, highlights the problematic nature of hidden acts. Hidden acts of disobedience of God's commands pose a special threat to the community, and they are punished by punishments so terrible that they reduce the people to doing acts that can only be done in hiding.

That the verse about the hidden and revealed things occurs at the end of the following chapter suggests that the meaning of "hidden" in this verse should be understood, as in the previous two chapters (chs. 27-28), as referring to acts that are hidden from the community. The verse concludes a chapter in which Moses has told the people that each and every member of the community is today standing before God to enter into a covenant backed by a curse, a covenant and curse that bind not only those present but future generations as well (29:9-14). The chapter goes on to warn that there may be a single individual, or a family, or a tribe who hears this curse but imagines in their heart that they will be spared from the curse—they believe that they can turn their hearts toward other gods and that they will not be punished (29:17-18). Nevertheless, God will punish that person or family or tribe and impose all of the terms of the curse on them (29:19-20). And, as the chapter continues, it seems that the entire nation will be punished for violating God's covenant, and the entire nation will be cast off their land because of God's wrath (29:21-27).

It appears then that, having entered into the covenant as a nation, the people's wellbeing can be compromised by the actions of even a single individual. And yet a community's ability to respond to the actions of an individual is limited—most especially, if that act is done in secret. And so this chapter concludes by saying that "the hidden things are for the Lord our God." Rashi explicitly links this to what has immediately preceded, offering a paraphrase of the reassurance that he understands God as giving to the people:

> And if you say: "What can we do?
> You are punishing the many for the thoughts of an individual—
> as it says:
> 'Lest there be among you a man [or a woman
> or a family or a tribe
> whose heart is turning today from the Lord our God]' (29:17)
> and afterwards:
> 'And they will see the plagues of that land
> [... which the Lord inflicted on it]' (29:21)—
> but surely no person knows
> the hidden things of their fellow!"
> I do not punish you for the hidden things,
> for they are "for the Lord our God" ... .
>
> Rashi on 29:28

Within its context in the book of Deuteronomy, then, the verse about the hidden and revealed things is responding to the terror of the curses that have been laid out in the previous chapters. (See Rashbam on 27:15 and Rav Yosef Kara on 27:26, who explicitly connect the verse about the hidden things to the curses of those who sin secretly in chapter 27.) Moses is asking the people to enter into a covenant with God, yet that covenant bears with it terrible curses for disobedience to God's word. And the community knows that there is no way that they can ensure that no one disobeys God's word or that, if someone does, the community will know about it and be able to punish that disobedience. The verse about the hidden things is meant to reassure the people: You do what you are able to do, responding to what you know about ("the revealed things are for us and our children"); I will take care of the hidden things and will not punish the community for those acts about which they do not know and to which they cannot respond ("the hidden things are for the Lord our God").

Each of the three interpretations of the hidden and revealed things that we have looked at addresses the problem of lack of knowledge with respect to sin and how a sin that is unknown impacts the individual or the community that has entered into a covenant with God. The first two interpretations raise critical issues about a person's ability to do right and, when they fail to do right, to set things right again. The third interpretation, which draws on the biblical context of the enigmatic verse, addresses the impact on a community of an individual's deeds of which the community is ignorant.

This interpretation is borne out in a narrative that appears in the book of Joshua, in a passage that makes explicit reference to the Deuteronomy passage about blessings and curses. It also stands at the heart of a striking talmudic dispute about the extent of a community's responsibility for the acts of each of its members, a dispute that the Talmud puts in conversation with the narrative from the book of Joshua. Both of these passages unsettle the reassurance that the verse in Deuteronomy appears to be offering, raising the possibility that a community is accountable even for the hidden deeds of one of its members. The scope of a community's responsibility and the conditions under which a community is responsible hinge, according to the talmudic passage, on how to understand the significance of the dots that appear above several of the letters in our verse.

THE DOTS

The verse about the hidden and revealed things is not the only biblical verse in which dots appear above some of the letters. Dots appear above words or letters in ten verses in the Torah and another five elsewhere in the Tanakh. The consensus of scholars is that these dots signify erasure; they indicate words or letters that existed within the manuscript tradition but that the transmitters of the text believed were erroneous. Classical rabbinic interpreters were aware of this meaning of the dots, as the *midrash* which introduces this essay makes clear: Ezra put dots above the words to indicate that the words should not be there. At the same time, since the words or letters marked by the dots are retained within the transmitted text, the dotted words were seen to be loci of interpretation, containing some kind of ambiguity or attenuation or hidden meaning.

The *midrash* about Ezra and our verse suggests that the verse can be read both *with* the dotted words and *without* the dotted words, and that Ezra is not sure which reading is correct. As transmitted to us, then, the verse contains two different meanings—while the *midrash* suggests that only one is correct and that Ezra is not sure which one that is, our reception of the verse includes both possibilities, a reading with the marked words and a reading without them. And, as it turns out, in this case the two readings are contradictory. How can we understand a verse that is transmitted to us with two contradictory meanings?

One possibility is suggested by a *midrash* on this verse that appears in the Talmud. The *midrash* accepts *both* readings, explaining the contradictory readings—one based on the verse including the marked words and one based on the verse with the marked words deleted—as referring to two different time periods:

> "The hidden things are for the Lord our God
> but the revealed things are for us and our children forever..."
> (Deuteronomy 29:28).
>
> Why are there dots above [the letters of]
> "for us and our children" and the *ayin* of "forever"?
> This teaches that [God] did not punish for the hidden things
> until Israel crossed the Jordan
> —the words of Rabbi Yehudah.
>
> Said to him Rabbi Nehemiah:
> But did [God] ever punish for the hidden things?!
> But it says: "forever"!
> Rather, just as [God] did not punish for the hidden things,
> so [God] did not punish for revealed sins
> until Israel crossed the Jordan.
>
> *Bavli Sanhedrin 43b*

Both Rabbi Yehudah and Rabbi Nehemiah (in some manuscripts, Rabbi Yose) take the two readings of the verse as referring to two different time periods, one before the Israelites crossed the Jordan River and one after. According to Rabbi Yehudah, before crossing the Jordan the people were punished only for "revealed things," but after crossing the Jordan they were punished for "hidden things" as well. Rabbi Yehudah's interpretation appears to be based on the understanding that the dots on the letters are deliberately misplaced—they appear above "for us and our children" and on the first letter of the next word, "forever," but they actually belong elsewhere in the verse (see Rashi and Tosafot). Indeed, it is exceptionally odd that there is a dot only on the first letter of the two-letter word *ad* (the first of the two words translated together as "forever"). Generally, dots appear either on entire words or on parts of words that can be deleted and still leave a meaningful lexical unit. (Genesis 18:9 is an exception, in which dots appear over three of the four letters in the marked word.) But erasing the first letter of the word *ad* would leave only a single letter, rendering the verse unreadable.

Rabbi Yehudah, apparently, believes that the dots—eleven in number— are meant to mark the words "for the Lord our God," which include eleven letters. Since it would not be appropriate to mark God's name for erasure, the dots are moved elsewhere in the verse, marking words that include ten letters and overlapping the beginning of the next word. The two readings of the verse, therefore, are generated by including or omitting the words "for the Lord our God." Here are the two readings of the verse; the parts of the verse that speak of the hidden things are in italics:

> *The hidden things are for the Lord our God*
> but the revealed things are for us and our children forever
> to do all of the words of this teaching.

> *The hidden things* and the revealed things
> *are for us and our children* forever
> to do all of the words of this teaching.

The first reading makes a sharp distinction between the hidden and the revealed things: while we are responsible for the revealed things, the hidden things are for God. This is the reading that was discussed above, reassuring the people that, though they stand before God and accept the covenant and the curse, they will not be held responsible for actions of an individual of which they are unaware. This, according to Rabbi Yehudah, describes the situation before the Israelites crossed the Jordan River.

The second reading, according to Rabbi Yehudah, describes the situation after the Israelites crossed the Jordan. This reading omits the reference to God, generating a completely different understanding of the verse's import: both the revealed things and the hidden things are *for us*. According to this reading, the people as a whole is held responsible for even the hidden things, actions of an individual of which they are totally unaware!

For Rabbi Nehemiah, this reading is untenable. It cannot be that God would ever punish the entire people for acts of which they are unaware. How precisely Rabbi Nehemiah interprets the dots is disputed among the commentators, but I think that the simplest explanation is that he takes them to be in their proper place. Thus, the words that are to be retained or deleted are "for us and our children." As for the eleventh dot—some manuscripts do not have the dot on the first letter of "forever," and perhaps Rabbi Nehemiah is working with this tradition. Alternatively, perhaps, as Rashi suggests, the dot on "forever" is taken to attenuate that word—not everything that the verse speaks about will remain forever as it always had been; rather, there will be a change at a point in time in one of the situations that the verse describes. In any case, here are the two readings of the verse, first retaining and then omitting the words "for us and our children":

> The hidden things are for the Lord our God
> *but the revealed things are for us and our children* forever
> to do all of the words of this teaching.
>
> The hidden things are *for the Lord our God*
> and *the revealed things* forever
> to do all of the words of this teaching.

The first reading is, of course, identical to the first reading according to Rabbi Yehudah. It takes the verse in its entirety, which makes a sharp distinction between the hidden and the revealed things. The second reading generates a contradictory reading, as did the second reading according to Rabbi Yehudah. But here the second reading does not make the people responsible for the hidden things. On the contrary, the people are not only never responsible for the hidden things—they are not even responsible for the revealed things! Both the hidden and the revealed things are "for the Lord our God." For Rabbi Nehemiah, the second reading refers to the period before the Israelites crossed the Jordan; at that time, they were responsible for neither the hidden nor the revealed things. After crossing the Jordan, though, they became responsible for the revealed things, as expressed in the first reading of the verse.

Both Rabbi Yehudah and Rabbi Nehemiah, then, understand the crossing of the Jordan to transform something about the responsibility of the people as a whole for the deeds of an individual. Before crossing the Jordan, they suggest, the people were not responsible for one another's actions—at least, according to Rabbi Yehudah, not for their hidden actions and even, according to Rabbi Neḥemiah, not for their revealed actions. But after crossing the Jordan into the promised land, the people become responsible, according to Rabbi Neḥemiah, for each other's revealed actions and, according to Rabbi Yehudah, even for each other's hidden actions.

Both of these positions align with the contextual reading of the verse about the hidden and revealed things in understanding the verse as addressing the challenge that an individual's secret acts pose for the community. But Rabbi Yehudah's reading undermines the assurance that the verse seems to be offering. While the verse seems to reassure the people that the curses attendant upon violating God's covenant will not devolve upon a community that is not aware of the evil deeds of one of its members, according to Rabbi Yehudah that reassurance expires when the people enter the promised land. After crossing the Jordan, he understands the verse with its marked letters to be saying, the people as a whole will indeed be held accountable for even the most secret actions of any of its individual members.

Rabbi Yehudah's claim is rejected out of hand by Rabbi Neḥemiah and indeed is hard to understand – how can anyone be held accountable for someone else's actions of which they are unaware? Yet the idea that a community suffers because of the hidden act of one of its members underlies a biblical narrative that takes place shortly after the Israelites cross the Jordan, the story of Akhan in the book of Joshua. In fact, the Talmud situates the dispute between Rabbi Yehudah and Rabbi Neḥemiah in the context of a discussion about that biblical narrative.

AKHAN AND THE BATTLE OF AI

The story of Akhan and the battle of Ai illustrates what it might look like for a people to be held accountable for the hidden actions of an individual. It raises critical questions about how we might understand this communal accountability and about what conditions of community might create this kind of shared responsibility.

The disastrous story of the battle of Ai immediately follows the miraculous victory at Jericho, the first city that the Israelites conquer in the promised land. Just before Jericho fell, Joshua declared all of the property of the city to be _ḥerem_—off-limits for human benefit (Joshua 6:17-18). But the following chapter begins with a notice that an individual named Akhan has, contrary to Joshua's prohibition, taken something from the _ḥerem_ (7:1).

After that brief notice, the narrative moves on to tell about the battle against Ai. Joshua sends scouts to Ai to gather information about how to conquer it, and the scouts report that the city will be easy to conquer. Joshua, they say, should not bother to send the entire people to fight Ai; two or three thousand fighters will be enough (7:2-3). Joshua sends about three thousand men to battle and, to the shock of the reader who has just learned of the miraculous and casualty-free conquest of Jericho, the soldiers flee and thirty-six men are killed. The people, newly arrived in the land of Canaan, are terrified and discouraged (7:4-5). Joshua tears his garments and, along with the elders of the people, falls on his face before the ark of the Lord. Joshua calls out to God and expresses his fear that the people will not be able to conquer the land and, instead, will be destroyed by the inhabitants of the land of Canaan (7:6-9).

At stake in the story of Ai, then, is whether the people will be able to possess the land toward which they have journeyed and which they have just entered. While Jericho was conquered easily, with neither a battle nor loss of life for the Israelites, the apparently easy-to-conquer city of Ai looms as a roadblock in the journey toward the Israelites' destiny. Something has gone wrong and, without it being set right, the people will fail in their effort to conquer and possess the land.

I want to focus on two aspects of the story that account for the failure at Ai: the relationship of the people as a whole to the sinner and his sin, and the nature of the sin that has been committed. In order for the Israelites to be able to move forward and come into possession of the promised land, they will need to address both of these issues.

> The Children of Israel committed a trespass
> regarding the _ḥerem_,
> and Akhan the son of Carmi the son of Zabdi the son of Zerah
> of the tribe of Judah took from the _ḥerem_,
> and the anger of the Lord burned against the Children of Israel.
>
> _Joshua 7:1_

The description of the taking of the *ḥerem*, which sets the stage for the story of Ai, alternates between talking about Akhan and talking about the nation as a whole. Akhan is described as the person who took from the *ḥerem*, and he is designated in the most specific of ways, by his own name and that of his father, grandfather, and great-grandfather, as well as of his tribe. At the same time, the verse begins by attributing the trespass to the Israelites as a whole, and it ends by speaking of God's anger against the entire people. Similarly, when Joshua falls on his face and appeals to God, God responds by describing the sin that has been committed as the act of the entire nation:

> Israel has sinned
> and also they have violated my covenant
> that I commanded them
> and also they have taken from the *ḥerem*
> and also they have stolen
> and also they have deceived
> and also they have put it among their possessions.
>
> Joshua 7:11

God, then, is treating this sin as a collective act, even though it is the sin of a single individual. The *ḥerem*, God tells Joshua, is *be-kirbekhem*—in your midst, literally inside you. The word appears three times in God's reply to Joshua and in God's instructions as to what Joshua is to say to the people. The people are understood to be a corporate entity, and the forbidden object has infected this entity. The people itself, God says, has become *ḥerem*; God will not remain with them, and they will not be able to stand before their enemies (7:12-13; see 6:18).

This is so even though, it appears, no one knew anything about Akhan's taking of the *ḥerem*. Joshua needs to be informed by God that someone has taken of the *ḥerem*, and he needs to be instructed by God to organize a lottery to determine who the sinner is (7:14). And yet, even though no one knows about Akhan's sin, the entire people is held responsible for this secret act and suffers its consequences.

The story's emphasis on the people as a corporate entity arises again in relation to the fighting force that is needed to battle Ai. The scouts had recommended to Joshua that "the whole people" not be sent to battle, and Joshua had followed their suggestion, sending only a small fighting force (7:3). But, after the episode of Akhan reaches its conclusion, God instructs Joshua to go to battle against Ai once more, this time taking with him "the whole people" (8:1). Similarly, once Akhan is discovered as the sinner and the misappropriated *herem* is found, the objects are brought to *all* of the Israelites (7:23), and *all* the Israelites participate in punishing Akhan (Joshua 7:25). The entire people, then, has to take responsibility for Akhan's act and obliterate the sinner from their midst, and the entire people has to join together in battle for possession of the promised land.

Most strikingly, immediately after Ai is finally destroyed, Joshua builds an altar, writes Moses's teaching on the stones, and performs the ceremony on Mount Gerizim and Mount Ebal. He reads all of the words of the Torah, the blessing and the curse, before the entire community of Israel. (8:30-35). And it is at this point, not after the miraculous battle of Jericho but after the battle of Ai and the ceremony that follows it, that the Canaanite kings understand that the people who have come to their land are poised to conquer and possess it (9:1).

"*Then* Joshua built an altar to the Lord God of Israel at Mount Ebal" (8:30). The narrative emphasizes the link between the story of Ai and the affirmation of the covenant and its blessings and curses on the two mountains. It is only *then*, after the community takes responsibility for the actions of an individual and after the people understand that they must all act together against both internal threats and external enemies, that the people's acceptance of the covenantal blessings and curses makes sense. As we saw, these blessings and curses and their elaboration in the succeeding chapters in Deuteronomy emphasize both corporate responsibility and the fear of hidden actions and their consequences. That fear becomes a reality in the story of Ai, where the covert sin of one individual, Akhan, poses a threat to the entire people.

AKHAN'S SIN

When Joshua asks Akhan to confess his sin, Akhan elaborates on what he has done:

> I saw among the spoils one good mantle of Shinar
> and two hundred silver shekels

and one bar of gold fifty shekels in weight,
and I desired them and I took them,
and behold they are hidden in the earth inside my tent,
and the silver under it.

Joshua 7:21

Akhan saw something that he wanted, and he took it, despite the fact that it was off-limits to him. This kind of act—seeing and taking what is off-limits—is the paradigmatic sin of the two children of Ham with whom the story of the Israelites intersects throughout the biblical narrative—the Egyptians and the Canaanites (Genesis 10:6). The Egyptians, for example, see Sarai and take her for Pharaoh (12:14-15). Shechem, the Canaanite prince, sees Dinah and takes her (34:2).

The Egyptians and Canaanites, in turn, are replicating the primordial sin of the first humans—Eve sees the fruit of the Tree of Knowledge and takes it for herself and for Adam (3:6)—as well as the sin of *benei ha-elohim*, who see the daughters of men and take them for themselves (6:2).

These two acts of seeing and taking in the primordial narrative propel humanity into the state of mortality, causing Adam and Eve to be cast out of Eden, so that the Tree of Life will be out of reach (3:22-24), and imposing a limit on the human lifespan (6:3). That Shechem later perpetrates this same sin in the land of Canaan manifests and portends the Canaanites' inability to remain in God's chosen place. The story of Shechem is replete with echoes of God's covenant with Abraham, in which God explains that Abraham's descendants will dispossess the Canaanites because of their sinfulness (15:16; compare 33:18 and 34:21). And the conquest of Canaan by the Israelites actually begins with the destruction of the city of Shechem by Jacob's sons in response to the prince's rape of their sister (ch. 34).

That living in the land of Canaan is predicated on rejecting the very sins that characterize the Canaanites and the Egyptians is made explicit in Leviticus:

Like the deeds of the land of Egypt
in which you have dwelt
you shall not do,
and like the deeds of the land of Canaan

> to which I am bringing you
> you shall not do… .

Leviticus 18:3

The land vomits out people who do such things; it will cast out the Canaanites, and the Israelites must eschew their behavior so that the land will not cast *them* out (18:24-28).

The promised land, then, is a kind of new Eden, a place which holds the promise of being in God's presence (26:3-12) and the threat of being cast out from God's presence (26:31-33). What makes the land available to the Israelites is the Canaanites' sin, and if the Israelites act similarly they will not be able to remain in possession of the land. And yet, at the very moment that the Israelites are to begin conquering the land, Akhan sees and he takes!

In fact, Akhan sees a mantle that is *good*, and he *desires* the objects that he sees. These two terms, along with *seeing* and *taking*, strongly evoke the sin that cast the first human beings out of Eden: Eve *saw* that the tree was *good* and *desirable*, and she *took* of its fruit (Genesis 3:6). The name Akhan might also suggest the word *ekhen/akhna* (attested in post-biblical Hebrew and Aramaic texts as a word meaning "snake"), again evoking the story of Eden, in which the snake tempts Eve to take the forbidden fruit, bringing about the expulsion of humanity from the Garden. Replicating the sin of Adam and Eve as well as the sin of the Canaanites, Akhan makes it impossible for the people to dwell in God's land.

In addition to *seeing* and *taking*, several other elements of the Akhan story recall the story of Shechem. The place at which Akhan is executed is the Valley of Akhor, Joshua declaring "Just as you troubled us (*akhartanu*), the Lord will trouble you (*ya'korkha*) this day" (Joshua 7:25). The valley's name echoes Akhan's own name; in fact, in Chronicles, Akhan is called Akhar, "the troubler (*okher*) of Israel" (1 Chronicles 2:7). The word "to trouble" had already appeared when Joshua declared the ḥerem: "Keep away from the ḥerem lest you become ḥerem; if you take from the ḥerem, you will make the camp ḥerem, and you will trouble (*va-akhartem*) it" (Joshua 6:18). Additionally, when God instructs Joshua how to identify and punish the person who took the ḥerem, God concludes "for he has violated (*avar*—perhaps another play on *akhar*) the Lord's covenant, and for he has done a disgraceful thing (*nevalah*) in Israel" (7:15).

These two words—"trouble" and "disgraceful thing"—both appear in the story of Shechem. Jacob's sons are distressed when they hear what Shechem did to their sister, "because he did a disgraceful thing (*nevalah*) in Israel" (Genesis 34:7). And Jacob chastises Simeon and Levi after the slaughter of the Shechemites, saying "you have troubled (*akhartem*) me" (34:30). The *nevalah* that Shechem perpetrates makes the Canaanites unable to remain in the land, and the *nevalah* that Akhan perpetrates makes it impossible for the Israelites to possess the land. (The fact that, in the Genesis story, it is Jacob's sons, not the Canaanites, who are accused of "troubling" is one of many features of that story that raise questions about the sons' behavior and whether even this early conquest of the land is tainted.)

Further, Akhan confesses that he has hidden the misappropriated objects inside his tent (Joshua 7:21). The hiddenness of the objects highlights the point made earlier about communal responsibility for hidden sins. In addition, the word used here, *temunim*, once again evokes the story of Shechem and its aftermath. Immediately after the conquest of Shechem, God instructs Jacob to go to Bethel, where Jacob had encountered God as he fled from Esau years earlier (Genesis 35:1). Jacob understands that, in order to go to Bethel—"*beit el*," the house of God (28:17-19)—his household has to divest of property associated with idolatry and idolatrous peoples (35:2). Members of Jacob's household give him the foreign gods and earrings in their possession, likely at least some of it booty that they had just captured from Shechem, and "Jacob hid (*va-yitmon*) them underneath the terebinth tree that is near Shechem" (35:4; to this divestment and placement under a tree, compare Joshua 24:23, 26). The tent inside which Akhan hides the *ḥerem* also echoes the Jacob story. While Jacob buries the divested object underneath *ha-eilah*, Akhan confesses that the objects that he has taken are hidden in *ha-oholi*, the Hebrew word for "tent" sharing the same three letters as the word for "terebinth." And so, while Jacob knows that he has to rid his household of tainted possessions in order to return to God's place and take possession of the land from people who have done a *nevalah*, Akhan does a *nevalah*, appropriating forbidden objects captured from the Canaanites and hiding them, not to divest of them but to keep them.

Two other details of the story underscore Akhan's assimilation to the family of Ham. One of the objects that Akhan sees and takes and hides is a mantle of Shinar. Shinar is the land of Nimrod, a descendant of Ham

(Genesis 10:8-10). And Akhan is condemned to the same fate that awaits the king of Ai—like the Canaanite king, Akhan is buried under a great heap of rocks (Joshua 7:26; 8:29).

It is noteworthy that Ai is near Bethel, the place to which Jacob will return after he divests of his family's tainted possessions. We are first introduced to Ai in the Tanakh when God calls to Abram and Abram travels to the land of Canaan and within it. God first appears to Abram in Shechem, where God promises to give the land to Abram's descendants (Genesis 12:7). Abram moves from there to a location east of Bethel: "with Bethel on the west and Ai on the east" (12:8). In the book of Joshua, Ai is also described as east of Bethel, but here it is linked to another place, called Beth-aven: Ai is "beside Beth-aven, east of Bethel" (Joshua 7:2). Bethel (*"beit el"*) is the house of God; Beth-aven (*"beit aven"*) is the house of iniquity. In fact, Hosea uses the name Beth-aven in mocking condemnation of Bethel (Hosea 4:15; 5:8; 10:5, 8). And Amos ominously declares: "Bethel will become Aven" (Amos 5:5).

Locating Ai in relation to both Bethel and Beth-aven, our story returns us to the moment at which Abram entered the land and the moment at which Jacob entered the land. Jacob had named the place at which he encountered God when he was fleeing Esau *"beit el,"* recognizing it as the house of God and declaring that, should he return in peace, the stone that he set up there would be the house of God (Genesis 28:17-22). Returning to the land many years later, Jacob is called by God to fulfill that vow. It is then that Jacob buries his family's divested objects, enabling the family to go to Bethel and to worship God there (Genesis 35:1-7). By situating Ai between Bethel and Beth-aven, our story signals that the events at Ai will be crucial in determining whether the Israelites will be able to enter God's land and build God's house or whether they will assimilate to the iniquitous behavior of the inhabitants of the land and so will be unable to dispossess them and dwell in the promised land.

The Hidden and the Revealed

THE HIDDEN THINGS ARE FOR US

That Akhan's sin has consequences for the entire people is an instantiation of the insight of Rabbi Yehudah and Rabbi Neḥemiah in their interpretations of the verse about the hidden and the revealed things: both sages aver that something changes in the nature of communal responsibility when the Israelites cross the Jordan into the promised land. Akhan's deed, the paradigmatic act of the Canaanites and of all those who cannot abide in God's special place, is not his deed alone. All of Israel is held accountable for the act of a single individual and, consistent with Rabbi Yehudah's position, this is so even though Akhan acted secretly and the objects that he misappropriated were hidden. Having crossed the Jordan, about to stand at Mount Gerizim and Mount Ebal, the people become responsible not only for the revealed things, but for the hidden things as well.

How can we understand the notion that everyone is held responsible for something that they know nothing about? One possibility is that the act of an individual says something about the community as a whole, even if other members of the community had no direct hand in the act and knew nothing about it. From this perspective, the individual is only able to do what they did because of something in the communal structure or culture that set the stage for their act. That might be because the community is structured in such a way that enables bad acts to be perpetrated. Or it might be because the individual is enacting something that is a feature of the community as a whole. These are quite different ideas, but they share the underlying assumption that there is something about the community itself that enabled the act. The community's responsibility for the act of the individual is grounded in the fact that the individual would not have done the bad act had the community been more perfectly organized or more fully infused with good values.

A second possibility is that everyone is held accountable even if they in no way can be seen to have enabled or contributed to the individual's act. All members of the community are held accountable, nevertheless, simply because they are members of the same community as the perpetrator of the bad act. Again, there are at least two versions of such a notion. One is that the community is held accountable not in the sense of having participated in the act, but in the sense that their fate is intertwined with the individual who has behaved badly. According to this understanding, the emphasis is not so much on the sinful act itself but on the *consequences* of the act. That is, the community is held accountable despite not being responsible for the commission of the act.

Alternatively, and most radically, perhaps the community is held to be responsible even for an act to which they did not actually contribute because the community is construed to have participated in the act by virtue of the nature of community. The person who committed the crime is a member of the community, and so the community has sinned and is held accountable for that sin. According to both versions of this second perspective, the community is not punished because of a causal relationship between the community and the commission of the crime. Rather, the community bears the consequences of the crime because of the cosubstantiality of the individual and the community. This perspective denies the autonomousness of the individual; all individuals are a part of a single community, and so all members of the community are responsible for the act of any member of the community—or rather, the community as a whole is responsible for any and all of its parts.

This second possibility, in both of its versions, is more difficult to understand than the first. The first possibility included an element of causality: the community has, in one way or another, made possible the act of the individual, and therefore the community shares in responsibility for the act that the individual has committed. But the second possibility denies this causal relationship between the community and the act of the individual. Instead, it posits a particular kind of relationship between the members of a community, a relationship that entails a shared communal fate or that implicates the entire community in the acts of each of its members.

I want to think through this second possibility by considering the rabbinic idea of *areivut*, a concept referenced by Rashi in his commentary on the talmudic text about the hidden and the revealed things. Rashi explains why the talmudic sages imagine that there was a shift in corporate responsibility when the Israelites crossed the Jordan: because it was then that the Israelites "heard and accepted upon themselves the blessings and the curses at Mount Gerizim and Mount Ebal and became responsible one for the other—*areivim zeh ba-zeh*" (Rashi on Sanhedrin 43b, s.v. *ad she-avru*).

Rashi is invoking the rabbinic principle *kol yisrael areivim zeh ba-zeh*, a statement that has come into contemporary parlance as "all Jews are

The Hidden and the Revealed

responsible for one another," encapsulating the notion that Jews need to look out for and care for each other. In context, though, the rabbinic statement has a different nuance. It appears in the Talmud as well as in a variety of midrashic texts in relation to a verse from the admonition in Leviticus: "They will stumble, each over his brother" (Leviticus 26:37). The rabbinic passages interpret *be-aḥiv* ("over his brother") as *be-avon aḥiv*—"through the sin of his brother"—understanding the stumbling in this verse as falling because a different member of the community has sinned (Sifra BeḤukkotai chapter 7:5; Bavli Sanhedrin 27b; Bavli Shevuot 39a; and parallels). Both times that the Talmud cites this exegesis, it limits the teaching to situations in which the person had the power to protest or prevent their fellow's bad act. Nevertheless, the principle suggests a wholesale mutual responsibility and, as we saw, Rashi cites it in relation to the teaching about the hidden things, situations in which no one has the power to protest or seek to prevent a bad action, because no one knows about it.

Rashi cites this principle as well in relation to a talmudic teaching about *mitzvot*. The Talmud teaches that a person who has already fulfilled their own obligation to say a blessing can nevertheless enable someone else to fulfill *their* obligation by saying the blessing for them, in their hearing (Bavli Rosh Hashanah 29a). Rashi explains this mechanism by citing the principle of mutual responsibility: "For behold, all of Israel are responsible for one another with regard to *mitzvot*" (s.v. *af al pi she-yatza*).

Other commentators follow Rashi's lead but elaborate on how they understand the application of this principle to helping someone fulfill their *mitzvah* obligation. Rabbeinu Yonah, hewing to the original meaning of this principle as relating to sin, explains that "he is a guarantor for them, and it is his responsibility to save them from sin, and to exempt them from [their obligation to fulfill] the *mitzvot*." Rabbeinu Yonah looks to the concept of a guarantor to clarify how the principle works: just as a guarantor is responsible to make sure that their fellow does not remain in debt, each person is responsible to make sure that their fellow has not neglected to fulfill their *mitzvah* obligation (Rabbeinu Yonah's commentary on the Rif Berakhot 12a). This interpretation takes the word *areivim*, translated as "responsible," to imply that each person is an *areiv*, a legal term meaning "guarantor." The principle, according to this understanding, means that "all Jews are guarantors for one another."

The Ritva takes this idea a bit further and adds an additional dimension to the concept of *areiv*. He explains: "Even though the *mitzvot* are imposed on each individual, behold all Jews are *areivim* for one another, and all of them are like one body, and like a guarantor (*areiv*) who pays their fellow's debt" (Ritva on Rosh Hashanah 29a). The Ritva focuses not on saving from sin but on serving as a guarantor to pay a debt: just as a guarantor is obligated to pay a debt if the debtor is unable to pay it themselves, each person is obligated to do a *mitzvah* on behalf of a person who is unable to do it themself. And so, even if I have already fulfilled my own *mitzvah* obligation, as the other person's guarantor I still have the responsibility to do the *mitvzah* on behalf of the other person if they cannot fulfill that obligation themself. Further, the Ritva offers an explanation of the basis of the idea of Jews serving as *areivim* for one another: "all of them are like one body." The Ritva is taking the word *areivim* as suggesting a mixture—all of Israel are mixed together, forming a single body. It is this intermingledness that serves as the foundation for *areivut*, the legal status of guarantor that each member of the group has toward the others.

The most striking formulation of the principle is offered by the Ran. Why can a person who has already fulfilled their obligation to say a blessing nevertheless say the blessing for someone else? "For behold, all Jews are responsible for one another with regard to *mitzvot* and, since their fellow has not fulfilled their obligation, they are like one who themself has not fulfilled their obligation" (Ran on the Rif, 8a). For the Ran, it is not merely that I am a guarantor for the other person's debt and so have an obligation to pay that debt if the other person cannot pay it themself. Rather, if the other person has not fulfilled their obligation, it is as if *I* have not fulfilled *my own* obligation!

How can we understand such a claim? I think that the Ran is inviting us to imagine what happened when we stood at Sinai in a particular way. It is not that each of us stood at Sinai and accepted the obligation to observe the *mitzvot*. It is not even that each of us stood at Sinai and accepted the obligation to observe the *mitzvot* as well as the responsibility to keep our fellows from transgressing and to help our fellows fulfill their *mitzvah* obligations (see Bavli Sotah 37b). Rather, the Ran might be suggesting, we didn't stand at Sinai as individuals at all. We stood at Sinai as a corporate entity, a single body who took upon itself the obligation to observe the *mitzvot*. This obligation in fact requires each of us to perform the *mitzvot*, but the obligation is not upon ourselves as individuals. Rather, each of us is a member of an obligated community; if one of the community's members has not fulfilled a *mitzvah*, then all members of the community cannot yet be considered to have fulfilled their obligation. Each shares in the obligation of all.

This understanding might be reflected in a variant of the talmudic saying preserved in a fragment from the Cairo Genizah (T-S NS 288.131). In place of the word *areivim*, the fragment has the word *me'uravin*, mixed: "All of Israel are mixed together with one another." This version offers an image of the community as a mixture, in which the boundaries between individual elements are blurred. In fact, the notion of a mixture might be embedded even in the more commonly attested version, *areivim*. As we have seen, it seems to underlie the Ritva's understanding of how one person can serve as a guarantor for another person: it is because "all of them are like one body" that one can fulfill the obligation that belongs to another. But the image of intermingledness suggested by the Genizah variant seems to me particularly useful as a visualization of the Ran's explanation of *areivut*. According to the Ran, I and my fellow are intermingled in relation to our obligations; neither of our obligations can be said to be exclusively mine or exclusively theirs. We are mixed together with one another as parts of a single entity, and therefore none of us is an individual agent responsible for our own obligations alone.

Above, I laid out several different ways to understand the teaching about communal responsibility for the hidden things, which Rabbi Yehudah believes came into effect when the Israelites crossed the Jordan River into the promised land. The first two presumed that, in some way, the community can be understood to have participated in or enabled the sin of the individual, even if they didn't know about it. But the second two suggested that it might be possible to hold the community accountable even if they neither enabled nor actually participated in the sin of the individual. The insights of the commentators that we have explored offer models of thinking about this latter vision of community. The Ran's notion of corporate responsibility for *mitzvot*, in particular, asserting that the entire community shares in the obligations of each of its members, might be taken to suggest that the entire community shares in the good or bad deeds of each of its members. That is, this view denies the notion that anyone shoulders the responsibility for their deeds alone; the community, by its very nature as a corporate entity, is responsible for any of its actions. "*Ḥata yisrael*," God tells Joshua—"*Israel* has sinned" (Joshua 7:11).

Alternatively, as suggested earlier, it might be that the community is held accountable not because of corporate *responsibility* but because of their shared fate. That is, even if the community is *not* held responsible for the commission of the act, it nevertheless shares in the consequences of the act. A passage in Vayikra Rabbah offers two metaphors that illustrate this idea:

> Ḥizkiyah taught: "Israel is a scattered sheep"
> (Jeremiah 50:17)—
> Israel is likened to a sheep:
> Just as a sheep,
> when one of its limbs is hurt, all of its limbs feel it,
> so too Israel:
> "Shall one person sin
> [and you will be wrathful against the whole community?]"
> (Numbers 16:22).
>
> Rabbi Shimon ben Yoḥai taught:
> It is like people who are on a ship,
> and one of them took a drill and began to drill beneath himself.
> Their fellow said to them:
> "Why are you doing this?"
> They said to them:
> "What do you care?
> Isn't it underneath myself that I am drilling?"
> They said to them: "Because you are flooding the ship on us!"
>
> *Vayikra Rabbah, ed. Margaliot, 4:6*

The first image offered in this *midrash* is of a body in pain. Israel is imagined as a sheep by Jeremiah, Ḥizkiyah says, because each member of the community is like part of a single body; if one part is injured, the entire body is in pain. Similarly, if a single member of the community sins, the entire community can be subject to God's wrath.

Rabbi Shimon ben Yoḥai offers a second metaphor, a group of people on a ship. Each person's fate is intertwined with the others, and so no one can take an action that endangers themselves without endangering all of the others as well. The person who drills a hole under their place imagines that it is no one else's business, but the others recognize, of course, that that person's action will bring down the entire ship with everyone on it. (See Tanna de-Vei Eliyahu Rabbah 12 [in some editions, 11], in which a similar metaphor is explicitly linked to *kol yisrael areivim zeh la-zeh* as well as to Joshua's recollection of the Akhan episode in Joshua 22:20. The Joshua verse also appears in relation to the metaphor of the sheep in Mekhilta de-Rashbi on Exodus 19:6.)

These metaphors are offered in relation to the words "If a person (*nefesh*) sins..." (Leviticus 4:2). The *midrash* goes on to show that the word *nefesh* is used in the singular to refer to the collective of all of Jacob's descendants (Exodus 1:5). *Nefesh*, then, is both the individual person and the communal body. Everyone, according to the *midrash*, is implicated in an individual's sin because, as members of a single body, everyone suffers the consequences of a single person's act. This is not a judgment that everyone is in some sense guilty or responsible; it is simply a corollary of community. If a community has a shared fate, then the actions of any part of that community affect the whole of the community.

UNTIL ISRAEL CROSSED THE JORDAN

As we have seen, both Rabbi Nehemiah and Rabbi Yehudah agree that it is at the moment that the Israelites cross the Jordan River that there is a shift in the communal consequences of sin. According to Rabbi Nehemiah, it is only then that the community suffers the consequences of revealed acts, and according to Rabbi Yehudah, it is then that the community suffers the consequences even of hidden acts. That is, according to Rabbi Nehemiah, before crossing the Jordan there was no communal responsibility even for acts that the community knew about. But, according to Rabbi Yehudah, the community was always held responsible for known acts; what changes at the Jordan is that now even hidden acts harm the entire community.

Why would it be that this level of communal responsibility comes into effect at the moment of crossing the Jordan? One possibility is that this shift has to do with the nature of the land itself. As we saw in the texts discussed in "Why Rain Comes From Above," the promised land is a place in which God is specially present and for which God has special concern. And, as we saw in the discussion above of the sins of the Canaanites and of Akhan, it is a land from which God casts out those who are sinful. Crossing over into the promised land, then, imposes a heightened responsibility on the people to ensure that no evil deeds are committed in their midst. And, as a people living as a nation on their own land, all members of the community are implicated in the sin of any of the community's members and suffer the consequences of the evil deeds that individuals do, even perhaps if they are done without the community's knowledge.

Alternatively, perhaps crossing over the Jordan is not about being in a particular land but rather about the Israelites becoming a nation to a fuller degree than before. The Israelites had been enslaved in Egypt together and redeemed from Egypt together, they had stood at Sinai together and traveled through the desert together. But it is crossing over the Jordan that propelled them into full nationhood. Being a nation entails the work of shaping a society that is responsible for all aspects of communal life. Having crossed the Jordan into the land that they will settle, the people for the first time constitute a polity. It is, perhaps, this new existence as a political entity, rather than the specific land into which the people has crossed over, that creates the heightened mutual responsibility of which the talmudic sages spoke. And certainly, if we focus not on responsibility but on consequences, living together as a nation heightens the degree to which everyone shares in the same fate. Whether one knows about the wrongdoing of another or not, whether the community can be held responsible for that wrongdoing or not, the fate of the entire nation is impacted by the actions of each of its members.

This latter perspective suggests the possibility of expanding the notion of *areivut* beyond *kol yisrael* ("all Israel" or "all Jews"). If shared responsibility in the strongest sense is a function of crossing the Jordan, and if crossing the Jordan means becoming a nation tasked with all of the elements of nation building and of sharing a common future, then it is arguable that all of us share responsibility and accountability within our national and local communities.

Perhaps we might think about *circles* of *areivut*, with different kinds and degrees of mutual and shared responsibility implied by different kinds and degrees of association. We share one kind of *areivut* with fellow Jews with whom we stood at Sinai and again at Mount Gerizim and Mount Ebal. But that *areivut*, rather than being exclusive, becomes a model for what it means to be a member of *any* community or nation. We are responsible for all things that happen within our community or nation, perhaps not only for the things that we know about but even for the things that are hidden from us.

"I PUT DOTS ABOVE THEM"

The *midrash* with which we began imagines Ezra the Scribe as being unsure about the correct reading of the verse from the book of Deuteronomy about which Elijah asks him. Ezra's puzzlement over this verse has echoed throughout time, as students of Torah have tried to make sense both of the dots above some of the letters and of the verse's obscure reference to hidden and revealed things. The dots, which signify erasure, generate both limited and expansive teachings about responsibility and accountability. And the words "hidden" and "revealed" point toward a variety of challenges related to the interplay between what we know and for what we are held responsible.

Some of these challenges relate to the inner world of the individual: Am I accountable for something that I did that I did not know is wrong? How can I atone for a wrongdoing that I do not know about? And others raise critical questions about the interplay between individual and community: about the challenges that an individual's acts pose for the community and about how the intensity of those challenges might vary as a community continues on its journey toward maturity.

This verse—and the ways in which it has been examined, interpreted, and illuminated within our biblical, liturgical, and rabbinic traditions—presents us with a complex set of tensions that are core to what it means to be a responsible human being and what it means to live within a society that strives to be good. The irresolvability of the verse demands that we struggle with these questions, and the alternative readings and understandings of the verse ground our thinking as we seek to take responsibility and to atone for our own actions and for the actions, past and present, of the communities of which we are a part.

ACKNOWLEDGEMENTS

I am grateful to Rabbi Elie Kaunfer for inviting me to publish this book with Hadar Press, and to Elisheva Urbas, Hadar's editorial director, for her meticulous reading and helpful suggestions. Many thanks also to Mikhael Reuven Kesher for his careful copyediting, and to Rachel Jackson of Binah Design and Dov Abramson of Studio Dov Abramson, for their beautiful interior and cover designs.

My appreciation to Rabbi Jon Kelsen for being a thought partner about religious imagination, and for calling to my attention Rabbi Kalonymus Kalman Shapira's teaching in Tzav ve-Zeruz, mentioned in the introduction to this volume. And thank you always to my lifelong conversation partner in Torah, Rabbi David Silber.

NOTES ON SOURCES AND SUGGESTIONS FOR FURTHER READING

INTRODUCTION

Tanya Luhrmann discusses the use of imagination in contemporary Evangelical Christianity and other religious traditions in *When God Talks Back: Understanding the American Evangelical Relationship with God* (Alfred A. Knopf, 2012) and *How God Becomes Real: Kindling the Presence of Invisible Others* (Princeton University Press, 2020).

WHY RAIN COMES FROM ABOVE

Umberto Cassuto's interpretation of rain and the *eid* in Genesis 2 appears in *A Commentary on the Book of Genesis, Part I*, trans. Israel Abrahams (Magnes Press, 1978), pp. 100–104.

I explore the understanding of rain reflected in Bavli Ta'anit in "Perception, Compassion, and Surprise: Literary Coherence in the Third Chapter of *Bavli Ta'anit*," *HUCA* 82-83 (2011-2012), pp. 61-117.

DARKNESS WILL ENVELOP ME

I first heard the insight that Hanukkah is at the darkest time of the year because of where it falls in the lunar cycle, in addition to its proximity to the winter solstice, in a lecture by Rabbi Yoel Bin Nun.

WORK AND ITS PURPOSES

Michael Fishbane highlights the centrality of the word "name" (*shem*) in the Tower of Babel story in *Text and Texture: Close Readings of Biblical Texts* (Schocken, 1979), pp. 37-39.

I discuss the Tower of Babel story in relation to the descendants of Ham and of Shem in *From Father to Son: Kinship, Conflict, and Continuity in Genesis* (Westminster/John Knox, 1991), pp. 144-145.

TO KNOW AND BE KNOWN

I discuss the contrast between Hagar and Abraham in Genesis 21-22 in *From Father to Son*, pp. 82-85.

For a discussion of the grouping of the ten plagues into three groups of three plagues, see Nahum M. Sarna, *Exploring Exodus: The Heritage of Biblical Israel* (Schocken, 1986), pp. 76-78. Rabbi David Silber points out that this grouping corresponds with the mnemonic acronym in the Passover Haggadah in *A Passover Haggadah: Go Forth and Learn* (Jewish Publication Society, 2011), pp. 50-51.

I first heard about the significance of the word *hitzil* at the beginning of the Exodus story as well as in the story of Jethro's visit from Rabbi David Silber.

Nahum Sarna discusses parallels between the description of the construction of the *mishkan* and the creation narrative in *Exploring Exodus*, pp. 213-214.

GOD'S ETERNAL ENEMY

Umberto Cassuto discusses the Song of the Sea in relation to ancient epic poetry and the myth of a primordial battle with the sea in *A Commentary on the Book of Exodus*, trans. Israel Abrahams (Magnes Press, 1974), pp. 177-181, and in "The Israelite Epic" in *Biblical and Oriental Studies, Volume II* (Magnes Press, 1975), pp. 69-109.

Notes on Sources and Suggestions For Further Reading

THE HIDDEN AND THE REVEALED

For a discussion of understandings of Deuteronomy 29:28 in rabbinic texts and Qumran, see Aharon Shemesh and Canna Werman, "Hidden Things and their Revelation," *Revue de Qumran* 18:3 (June 1998), pp. 409-427.

For discussion of the dotted letters in the Torah in relation to ancient scribal practices, see Romain François Butin, *The Ten Nequdoth of the Torah: Or the Meaning and Purpose of the Extraordinary Points of the Pentateuch* (J. H. Furst Company, 1906) and Emanuel Tov, *Scribal Practices and Approaches Reflected in the Texts Found in the Judean Desert* (Brill, 2004), pp. 202-204.

I discuss the Dinah story in relation to the patriarchal covenant and the conquest of the land of Canaan in *From Father to Son*, pp. 136-143.

For further discussion of the concept of *areivut*, see Reuben M. Rudman, "Kol Yisrael Areivim Zeh Ba-Zeh," *Tradition: A Journal of Orthodox Jewish Thought* Vol. 42, No. 2 (Summer 2009), pp. 35-49, and Aharon Lichtenstein, "Mutual Responsibility in a Jewish State," 2007 (https://www.etzion.org.il/he/halakha/studies-halakha/laws-state-and-society/mutual-responsibility-jewish-state). The relevance of crossing into the land for the parameters of mutual responsibility is discussed by Rabbi Lichtenstein and, more recently, by Tzvi Novick in "Land or Torah: What Binds Israel as a Nation?" *thetorah.com*, May 27th, 2020 (https://www.thetorah.com/article/land-or-torah-what-binds-israel-as-a-nation).

www.ingramcontent.com/pod-product-compliance
Lightning Source LLC
Chambersburg PA
CBHW060526080526
44586CB00012B/637